Numerology

Master the Divine Meaning of Numbers and
Discover Your Future Through Numerology,
Astrology and Tarot Reading

(Discover the Secret of Universe Using Zodiac
Signs, Wiccan Magic & Third Eye)

Saffi Strayhorn

Published by Rob Miles

© **Saffi Strayhorn**

All Rights Reserved

Numerology: Master the Divine Meaning of Numbers and Discover Your Future Through Numerology, Astrology and Tarot Reading (Discover the Secret of Universe Using Zodiac Signs, Wiccan Magic & Third Eye)

ISBN 978-1-989990-41-4

All rights reserved. No part of this guide may be reproduced in any form without permission in writing from the publisher except in the case of brief quotations embodied in critical articles or reviews.

Legal & Disclaimer

The information contained in this book is not designed to replace or take the place of any form of medicine or professional medical advice. The information in this book has been provided for educational and entertainment purposes only.

The information contained in this book has been compiled from sources deemed reliable, and it is accurate to the best of the Author's knowledge; however, the Author cannot guarantee its accuracy and validity and cannot be held liable for any errors or omissions. Changes are periodically made to this book. You must consult your doctor or get professional medical advice before using any of the suggested remedies, techniques, or information in this book.

Upon using the information contained in this book, you agree to hold harmless the Author from and against any damages, costs, and expenses, including any legal fees potentially resulting from the application of any of the information provided by this guide. This disclaimer applies to any damages or injury caused by the use and application, whether directly or indirectly, of any advice or information presented, whether for breach of contract, tort, negligence, personal injury, criminal intent, or under any other cause of action.

You agree to accept all risks of using the information presented inside this book. You need to consult a professional medical practitioner in order to ensure you are both able and healthy enough to participate in this program.

Table of Contents

INTRODUCTION 1

CHAPTER 1: METHOD 6

CHAPTER 2: HOW NUMEROLOGY WORKS 25

CHAPTER 3: THE NINE APPROACHES 33

CHAPTER 4: WHERE DID NUMEROLOGY COME FROM? ... 44

CHAPTER 5: THE SIGNIFICANCE OF THE NUMBERS 48

CHAPTER 6: TRIANGLE OF ENLIGHTENMENT 57

CHAPTER 7: THESE NUMBERS CASHED IN ON THE PROPERTY MARKET. YOU CAN TOO! 62

CHAPTER 8: THE COSMIC CLOCK OF GEMINI 73

CHAPTER 9: MASTER NUMBERS 11/2, 22/4, AND 33/6.... 94

CHAPTER 10: THE DESTINY NUMBER AND WHAT IT MEANS 113

CHAPTER 11: MASTER NUMBERS 128

CHAPTER 12: BUDAN – MERCURY (NUMBER 5) 136

CHAPTER 13: TAKE CONTROL OF YOUR LIFE 145

CHAPTER 14: WHEEL OF FORTUNE 153

CHAPTER 15: THE PRINCIPLES BEHIND PREDICTIONS..... 175

CHAPTER 16: KARMIC LESSONS 180

CHAPTER 17: USING YOUR NUMBERS TO WIN! 193

CONCLUSION... 194

Introduction

Numerology is a method of analyzing human personality and character traits, behavioral patterns, and past and future influences in one's life by using the birthdate. The method I use centers on the day of the month you were born for personality and compatibility analysis. I see the Birthday number as the real personality and essence of one's being.

Next, I sum up the numbers of the month, day, and year to a single digit to get what I refer to as the Facade number, or how the world sees you.

5 + 6 + 1923 = 17 = 8 Facade

Finally, I add and subtract the day, month, and year of birth in different combinations for analyzing past and future influences and trends from the womb to the grave, in the same way that astrologers use the natal and progressed chart wheels.

Going "strictly by the numbers," and by correlating the numbers to planets, I pinpoint specific aspects in a person's astrological chart without the time or place of birth. Of the most common forms of metaphysical readings, Tarot cards, palmistry, astrology, and pure psychic readings are the most popular because people are more familiar with them.

Since the early 1970's, much has been written about connecting with "higher forces," channeling back to the past to find one's place in the present, preparing for the "new age" and, in the end, has little or nothing to do with day-to-day living. This book offers real information for the everyday world and was written in the same way I give individual readings, direct and to the point. It will provide you with a solid, basic frame of reference for numerological readings. Through birthdate numbers, I've pinpointed trends and experiences in the lives of clients that their closest family members did not know. This book is the distillation of my understanding of the influence of numbers and astrology gained from over 20 years' experience reading for clients and friends, and also by studying the numbers of public figures, current events, as well as natural and man-made disasters. Some of the insights into human nature came to me during readings as intuitive flashes, but they were substantiated by feedback from clients.

Only about one numerological chart in a thousand pops up at me as a key to fulfilled expectations through minimum effort. However, having too easy a life often leaves one without the ability to cope with losses. No number combination is ideal, much less perfect. Happiness and conflict are integral and necessary components in everyone's lives and in all relationships, whether they are business, political, casual, family or romantic. All numbers and number combinations have positive and negative aspects, assets and liabilities.

The positive aspects of a numerological chart do not guarantee a free ride of any sort, and the negative aspects do not condemn people to any behavior or condition. Numbers combine to create the individual's personality and particular challenges. It is friction that moves the universe, gets us from Point A to Point B, and causes us to think and innovate. Imperfection is the child of Mother Nature and Father Time. Half the qualities of an individual or a relationship come from the number makeup. The other half comes from working through the weak areas and maximizing the strengths of those numbers. Personal choice always is first and last in anyone's life, and this text will show you how to use the emotional and intellectual style of your number makeup to balance the positive and negative parts of your number combinations. You will see the numerological basis for why experience and how trauma affects people in different ways and why some people go through life less affected by their past than those people who become a bundle of neuroses. I also explain the neurological basis for the variety of personal changes with age, why some people are late bloomers while others slow down with age.

Chapter 1: Method

Eleven numbers are used in numerology (1, 2, 3, 4, 5, 6, 7, 8, 9, 11 and 22: some numerologists also use 33). Each number represents different characteristics and expressions. Master numbers (11 and 22) are the exception to the rule of reducing to a single digit.

You add the digits of larger numbers together until the sum achieved is one of the core numbers above.

For example, instance if a calculated number is 19 it is reduced in this way:

1 + 9 = 10

1 + 0 = 1 making the number to be considered 1.

The exception is if your result gives a **master number** of 11, 22 or 33, which have their own special meanings. They are intensified versions of the single digit number they replace, and suggest potential for a high degree of learning and achievement. Sometimes master numbers can operate at a much more tangible or practical level, becoming essentially the same as the single digit.

There are no inherently good or bad numbers. Each number has both positive and negative connotations. They describe trends and possibilities and you are always able to make changes.

Pythagorean numerology assigns the number value by the sequence of the Western alphabet. The numbers are in sequence so you don't need to memorise the associations.

a	b	c	d	e	f	g	h	i
j	k	l	m	n	o	p	q	r
s	t	u	v	w	x	y	z	

Pythagoras believed that everything in the universe operates in predictable cycles based on natural law, and these cycles can be understood through the study of numbers. Number 1 is the symbol of unity, stability, and wisdom while 2 symbolises duality, polarity, and darkness. Under the Pythagorean system, even numbers are accepting/negative/female and odd numbers active/positive/male.

Some numerology numbers are valid throughout your life, whereas others are only relevant for a defined period.

One is the symbol of unity and often symbolises God or the universe, the fundamental unit from which all things had been created. The primary meaning of 1 is pure energy and beginnings. It represents both physical and mental activity. The number of origin and creation, 1 shows a capacity and potential to make a comeback after experiencing drawbacks. It is mainly related to fame rather than wealth. When it appears, 1 signifies you need to learn how to stand alone, be assertive, and achieve recognition for your talents. A 1 person is an achiever and prefers to be the centre of attention.

Keywords: Initiating; pioneering; leading; independent; attaining; individual; original; courageous; strength.

Gifts: Self-sufficiency; invention; mastery.

Challenges: Stubbornness; egotism; bluntness; ambition; dominance; wilfulness; impulsiveness.

Goal: Establishing individuality; making a name.

Fears: Being overlooked; not using talents.

Two is the first feminine number and represents the dualistic nature of the universe. It is often associated with negatives, as in the words 'duplicity' and 'two-faced'. The number 2 is intuitive and corresponds to our protective instincts. It symbolises the principle of coming together with another. A 2's individual achievements may not be realistic because they do best through co-operation and teamwork. Two people are usually supportive and diplomatic. As a 2, you're aware of others' needs as well as your own, and strive to demonstrate friendliness, understanding and tact. The number 2 can be represented by a balance, a desire to see both sides of any situation. Negatively, 2 can be grasping, overprotective and cranky.

Keywords: Co-operation; adaptability; consideration; mediation; empathy; over-sensitivity; co-dependence; service; harmony; patience; adaptability; peace maker; insightful; sensitive; diversity; conflict; dependence; artistic; shy; thorough; analytical.

Gifts: Charm, understanding, supportiveness, loving.

Challenges: Self-consciousness, fear, hesitation, over-conscientiousness, details.

Goal: Reciprocal relationships; security.

Fears: Unknown, unplanned change, being alone, making a mistake.

Three relates to expansiveness and learning through experience. It's often seen as a lucky number, and associated with money and good fortune. Three depicts people joining together to achieve a common goal. It also represents communication of all kinds. Negatively it can demonstrate pessimism, foolhardiness and unnecessary risk taking. Three has the power of growth and contains a beginning, middle and end, the past present and future, and is a complete cycle unto itself. It is a number of progress and expansion. If you are a 3 person, you are optimistic and fun-loving.

Keywords: Expression; sociability; superficiality; wastefulness; optimism; visionary; humorous; energetic; spontaneous; fun; wisdom; understanding; morality; spirituality; enthusiasm.

Gifts: Enthusiasm, imagination, versatility.

Challenges: Exaggeration, lack of direction, unfinished projects, sensitivity to criticism, laziness.

Goal: Enjoy life, stay young, play.

Fears: Loss of youth, restriction, boredom,

Four symbolises the principle of putting ideas into form and signifies work and productivity. It is the number of stability and building for the future. If you are a 4 person, you're constructive, and cautious. You direct much of your energy towards achieving your goals. Four represents progression and growth, and so you may come up with original ideas from nowhere. It is a solitary number and often indicates a loner. As a 4 you tend to be steadfast and may risk being boring.

Keywords: Foundation; order; service; struggle against limits; steady growth; practical; patient; logical; hard-working; loyal; steadfast; frugal; responsible; rigid; traditional; straightforward; reliable.

Gifts: Concentration, realistic values, system.

Challenges: Rigidity, too cautious, limited viewpoint.

Goal: Accomplishment, security.

Fears: Sudden change, deprivation, loss.

Five represents service to others. It's analytical with the ability to think critically, but can over think an issue. It governs our ability to think clearly and our intellectual capacity and represents our openness to new ideas. A 5 is likely to be an adventurer. Five is about pushing life to its limits. Five symbolises multiplicity, progression, and passion. It is the most deceitful and opportunistic of all the numbers. A 5 needs change, variety and growth. You constantly disseminate information and ask questions. You are attracted by the physical senses and indulgences.

Keywords: Expansiveness; vision; adventure; change; exploration; variety;

sensuality; unattached; curious; experienced adaptability; travel; inconsistency; abuse of senses; activity; influence; flair; intelligent; shrewd; cunning' diplomatic; pragmatic; opportunistic; persuasive; daring; non-conventional; unpredictable.

Gifts: Resourceful, magnetic, motivated, competitive.

Challenges: Restlessness, procrastination or activity with no direction, lack of follow through.

Goal: To win, to experience life to the maximum.

Fears: Growing old, not seeing the world, boredom.

Six is a number of beauty and attraction. It symbolises the principles of nurturing, caring, and harmony. As a 6, you need stability and a solid, comfortable home base. You make a good teacher, trainer or and parent. Sixes are happiest in conventional or familiar surroundings and can be opinionated and frugal or anxious when insecure. If you are a six, you're may take on the burdens of others unnecessarily. You are a lover of tradition, and health-oriented. Six is considered to be a minor money number, so a little extra income will be available wherever this number is found.

Keywords: Responsibility; protection; nurturing; community; balance; sympathy; harmony; beauty; love; marriage; family; understanding; meddling; jealousy; careful; teacher; conventional; provider; healer; unfaithful; jealous; charm.

Gifts: Caring, ability to compromise, reliability.

Challenges: Anxiety, being over controlled, co-dependency, guilt.

Goal: To provide for others' well-being, to create security and harmony, to love and be loved.

Fears: Lack of resources and love; world going to hell.

Seven is associated with the new and foreign. It has a philosophical touch in everything it does. It symbolises the need to find depth, meaning, and spiritual connection. If you are a 7 you need solitude in which to find the inner voice. You tend to be different, eccentric, or a loner and are very discriminating in all areas. Seven is a spiritual number and is thought of as being generally lucky. As a 7 you probably operate on a different wavelength and can be difficult to understand as well as get to know. You're happy to bombard everyone with questions but not so happy answering them. Needing to analyse everything can create a distance between you and others, and a fear of betrayal makes you keep people at a distance.

Keywords: Analysis; understanding; knowledge; awareness; wisdom seeker; reserved; inventor; deep-thinker; spirituality;; fault finding; suppression; specialist; loner; eccentric; thoughtful;

accurate; broadminded; introspective; distrustful; antisocial; impersonal; detached; psychic awareness; deceptive; insincere.

Gifts: Mental understanding, analysis, perfection.

Challenges: Pride, narrowness, distance, rigidity, connection to the past, argumentative, temper, silence.

Goal: To maintain control over life; to understand.

Fears: Failure to achieve standards, making a mistake.

Eight is a number of either success or failure and has no middle path. It is the most unfortunate number in the sense that it's always misunderstood. It is the number of loneliness and melancholy. Eight symbolises domination, control, and achievement and is the executive decision-maker. As an 8 you tend to be hard-headed. You're more comfortable in the realm of material, tangible facts. Eight people are good leaders although they many need to learn compassion. Your reputation and community standing are of paramount importance to you. Eight represents hard work and lessons learned through experience, and can be difficult because of the restrictiveness of its nature. More than any other number, eight seeks money and material success. Reversals in life are common for the eight.

Keywords: Practical; status oriented; materialistic; leader; achievement; abundance; self-disciplined; power; success; authority; unscrupulousness; formal; stern.

Gifts: Decisiveness, courage, focus, delegation.

Challenges: Belligerence, manipulation, anger, judgment.

Goal: To exercise control over environment, to achieve power and status.

Fears: Loss of prestige, being at the mercy of circumstances or of others less capable.

9

Nine is a number of domination, control, degeneration and destruction. It never tires of fighting. Nine symbolises the principle of a universal philosophy or consciousness. As a 9, you're a dreamer and at home in the realm of the arts, medicine, religion, drama, and philosophy and metaphysics. You're a healer and educator, acting always for the benefit of others. Nines look for solutions from the inspirational, intuitive, and creative worlds. Its energy is loving, compassionate, diffuse and global.

Keywords: Humanitarian; selfless; creative expression; compassionate; romantic; generous; philanthropic; loving; wisdom; idealist; romance; emotionalism; dissipation; generalist; multi-talented; teacher; healer; humanitarian.

Gifts: Understanding, communicating, influencing

Challenges: Drifting, tolerance, losing focus, bad habits

Goal: To make an impact in a big way; expansion.

Fears: Restriction of any kind, losing control of emotions.

The master numbers possess more potential than other numbers. They are highly charged, difficult to handle, and require time, maturity, and effort to integrate into your personality. Each master number provides its own form of service to humanity. With a master number, you have unlimited potential, and many believe a more developed soul. However, if you use your power selfishly it will be destructive.

11 Master Philosopher

Its intention is to provide illumination. You have a high degree of inner wisdom and a charisma that draws others to you. You are able to teach and advise others and may have psychic abilities. Eleven is the most intuitive number and represents a channel to the subconscious, insight, nervous energy, shyness, and impracticality. Eleven people are dreamers. Within it, 11 has all the aspects of two, with added charisma, leadership, and inspiration. The number 11 colours everything with drama, a visionary outlook and artistic sensitivity. It is not very practical but has a unique perspective and philosophy. Because 11 is so idealistic, you may appear unstable. The duality of 11 can create inner conflict. When it's not focused on a goal beyond itself, it can be turned inward to create fear and phobias. It is the psychic's number.

Keywords: Intuition; idealism; insensitive; fanatic; inspiration; inventiveness; spiritual; teacher; romance; artistic abilities; energy; enthusiasm; vision; moral courage; powerful; intuitive; prophetic; unfeeling; unstable; seeker of revenge; highly-strung; intense; polarised; subtle distant; detached; treachery.

Gifts: Revealing higher truths, transformation, poetic interpretation, romance

Challenges: Illusion, isolation, allergies, over-stimulation.

Goal: Living the dream.

Fears: Drudgery, restriction, ugliness, boredom.

22 Master Builder

Its intention is to build something tangible on a great scale. You have the dream that brings together the people and resources you need to make your dreams reality. A 22 person often seems ahead of their time. You are quick witted, far-sighted and intuitive, interested in anything new or revolutionary. This is a number of high idealism, wanting the best for the world and able to see the best the world has to offer. With a 22 you can turn the most ambitious dreams into reality. This is potentially the most successful of all numbers.

Keywords: Idealistic; expansive; visionary; government; universal transformation; philanthropic; large endeavours; powerful force; creative; inspired; spiritual; bigoted; revolutionary; practical idealism; material mastery; get-rich-quick schemes; viciousness; big ideas.

Gifts: Inspire others, common sense, intuition, practical.

Challenges: To share your vision and allow others to make contributions.

Goal: To be able to integrate seemingly conflicting characteristics within yourself- your inspiring vision and natural tendency toward practicality.

Fears: Loss.

33 Master Teacher

Not all numerologists recognise thirty-three as a master number.

Its intention is to communicate knowledge. You find original ways to encourage learning and are at the forefront of the search for truth. Thirty-three combines eleven and twenty-two, bringing their potential to another level. It lacks personal ambition, and focuses its abilities toward the spiritual uplifting of humanity. This is shown in a determination to seek understanding and wisdom before preaching to others. It is rare to experience thirty-three in its full force. Thirty-three is only important when found among the core numbers: In other cases it should be reduced to 6.

Keywords: Christ-like; healer; compassionate; blessing; teacher of teachers; martyr; monk; sincere devotion.

Gifts: Honesty, discipline, bravery.

Challenges: Requires self-sacrifice, courage.

Goal: Searching for the truth.

Fears: Lack of resources and love.

Chapter 2: How Numerology Works

Of all arts, numerology is the simplest to know and use. To reveal the magic of the numbers, all that is required is your complete birth date and your full names. The numerology numbers are arranged in a chart made up of nine single digits core numbers, which include 1, 2, 3, 4, 5, 6, 7, 8 and 9 and master numbers are 11, 22 or 33. Each of these numbers signifies special expressions and characteristics.

How To Use The Numbers In Your Date Of Birth

When using the numbers in your birth date, begin by expressing it numerically in the format mm/dd/yyyy

General Steps

1. Add the numbers in your full birth date or the values given to letters in your full name to form larger numbers. For example, lets calculate using October 12

1984 as the birth date. Add the digits in year first (1984), 1+9+8+4 which equal 22. Then add the digits in the month, (10th month; October), 1+0 which equals to 1. Finally add the digit in your date (12), 1+2, which equals 3.

2. Add all the answers you have gotten from adding the digits in your birth year, month, and date, that is, 22+1+3. If you get a larger figure or one that is not found on the chart like 26 in this case, you will need to reduce it further by adding 2+6, which will give you 8. For this case, number 8 is a core number so we stop here. The result you get in your final answer is the core number you will use to discover yourself.

Or;

Add up the digits of the large figures continually if necessary until you attain a master numbers 11, 22, or 33. Master numbers are not reduced further and are seen to be highly intense versions of number 2, 4 or 6. Master numbers indicate a higher learning or achievement potential in an environment that is more stressful. They operate in a more practical or tangible level in most people and are basically similar to the other single digits in the chart. For example, let's use January 2nd 1990 to illustrate a possible scenario. If you add (1+9+9+0) + (2) + (1), you get 22, which is a master number so use it as it is without reducing its value further. Same case applies if you get 11 or 33.

How To Use Your Full Name

You can also use your full names to work out the numbers using a numerological chart with numbers assigned to each letter in the English alphabets.

Here is the chart

1	2	3	4	5	6	7	8	9
A	B	C	D	E	F	G	H	I
J	K	L	M	N	O	P	Q	R
S	T	U	V	W	X	Y	Z	

*Note; only use the name recorded on your birth certificate for all calculations that require your name. No nicknames or changed names including your marriage name in order to avoid interfering with the calculations. Suffixes such as Sr. or Jr. are also not included.

General Steps

1. Write down your name and assign each letter a number in reference to the chart above.

2. Add all the digits obtained and there you have your core number!

You can now come up with various numerological calculations using the numbers obtained. Just to mention a few, have a look at the following:

Life Path Number

Your life path number gives amazing details about your personality, career, jobs, wealth, and successes. To calculate your life path number, use your date of birth. To help you understand better, let's take October 12 1984 as the birth date example.

Steps by step instructions

To start, add all the digits in year of birth together; for instance, using the example take 1984, add 1+9+8+4, which equals to 22.

Now, if your day of birth contains more than one digit, add up all the digits in it. For instance, take 12; add 1+2, which equals to 3.

Then add up all the digits in your month of birth. For instance, October is the 10th month; add 1+ 0 which equals 1.

Add up all the answers you got from step 1, 2, and 3. For instance, add all the three digits obtained, 22+3+1, which totals to 26.

To get our final answer, add the digits in step 4 answer. That is 2+6 in this case, which gives us 8.

Your final answer (8 for this case), is the most important number in your life, and influences your life path.

Expression/Destiny Number

This number describes your inborn abilities, natural talents, inner goals, and opportunities at your disposal. It is calculated by converting all the letters in your full name into numbers using the chart provided earlier.

In order to make it easier for you, let me give some few tricks:

Put the numbers assigned to the vowels above the name and those of the consonants below. With the exception of Y which can be classified as a consonant or a vowel. For example, in the name Yolanda, Y is a consonant but in Larry, it's a vowel. This will make it easier to derive the soul urge number.

For example taking the name Larry James King

	1			7	1		5			9		
L	A	R	R	Y	J	A	M	E	S	K	I	N	G
3		9	9		1		4		1	2		5	7

Vowel addition is 1+7+1+5+9=23

Consonants addition is 3+9+9+1+4+1+2+5+7=41

Step by step guide

1. Write down your name in full.

2. Add up all the numbers assigned to vowels in the top row.

3. Add up all the numbers assigned to the consonants in the bottom row.

4. Take the answer you get from adding the vowels and add it to the answer you get from adding the consonants i.e. 41+23 then sum up the totals to get 64 in this case.

5. Reduce the number by adding 6+4 to get 10. The number 10 is not among the core numbers so reduce it further by adding 1+0, which will give you a final

answer i.e. 1 then use this as your expression number for getting your reading.

Soul Urge Number

Your soul urge number signifies your heart's desire. It indicates what you crave to have and do in life.

Steps

Add all the numbers assigned to the vowels in your name. For example, 1+7+1+5+9 equals 23

Reduce the answer you get if necessary. That is 2+3=5. Use your final core number in your calculations to get your reading, 5 in this case.

The next chapter will show you the meanings of the core numbers in numerology.

Chapter 3: The Nine Approaches

How you learn depends greatly on your personality. Although we were all taught in school the standard approach to learning, which is from bottom to top, the truth is: we all have our own style. Some learners, for example, enjoy learning with periods of rest in-between; some others, on the other hand, do much better when they are given space and privacy to focus; some enjoy learning in groups; and some even enjoy learning while being nestled in their favorite chair, so on, and so on. When you allow yourself to think outside the box, you can come across so many ways to accommodate your learning experience. In this chapter, you will be introduced to nine approaches that will help you whenever you feel the need to improve your learning habits. Feel free to test them and combine them to make your own.

Approach 1:

Power Through

Set a timer to give yourself a sense of urgency. This approach emphasizes your fight and flight instincts. To learn or to fail. To win or to lose. There is only one answer and, of course, the answer is... to learn and win. If you are someone who easily becomes worried when learning, there is a chance you might be overthinking it. Tap into your natural instinct and focus on accomplishing one thing at a time. This approach promotes the tunnel vision mindset while it discourages multitasking. Be it ten pages of a text manual, a new language, or whatever it is you need to learn, power through as if your life is on the line. The key here is to keep moving forward and avoid stalling. If you have a lot of information to retain, go over the whole content to get a general idea of each section, then go back to the beginning to start over. Focus on each section one at a time. This approach helps anyone who has difficulty getting started but has no problem keeping the ball rolling once they get momentum.

Approach 2:

Find Support

Do you know someone who has the ability to motivate or inspire you to learn? Who is the first person that crosses your mind? It can either be a friend, a tutor, a coach, or even your neighbor. Take a moment to think about such a person. There is always someone you can reach out to if you give it some thought. Try to imagine how they would approach things themselves if they were you. If you are the type of person who lacks assertiveness and depends on guidance, tapping into someone's positive attitude can help you develop more successful habits. Ideally, you would want to be around them during your learning process; that way they can help you when you get stuck. Pick up the phone, dial a number, get an approval, and make it happen. Regardless of what you are trying to learn, it will all suddenly seem easier once you decide to take that one single step forward to find support.

Approach 3:

Explain It

Albert Einstein once said "If you can't explain it to a six year old, you don't understand it yourself." Whenever you get your mind off the details and focus on expressing yourself, just for the sake of it, you will realize how much you actually know. Make it a habit to explain what you have learned to a friend. Make a point. Allow your mind to quickly find ways to rearrange your thoughts so it can become clearer not only to your listener but also to yourself. Just allow your mind to relax and trust your power of expression. Like a child, dare to be creative and don't be ashamed if you lose your trail of thoughts. As you make it a habit to explain things to others, you reinforce the bridge between your conscious and subconscious mind; making it easier for your thoughts to turn into words.

Approach 4:

Make A Commitment

Some individuals just need to slow down and make a commitment. Before you start your day, do a brief ten minutes of meditation to get yourself in the right mindset. Make it a habit to deepen your breath and ground yourself. Staying grounded is the beginning to any kind of commitment. Progress will seem slow and dull but to approach learning progressively in a step by step fashion has always been the most reliable and effective way to learn. Adopt this approach and you are guaranteed to have a solid and reliable stepping stone to fall back on if ever anything were to happen.

Approach 5:

Make It Exciting

The idea of being glued to a chair for hours, with your toes going numb and your brain overloading beyond capacity is terrifying; and it can prevent you from learning truly wonderful things. But who says learning has to be a dreadful experience? Sure, that is the traditional way of going about it, but really, if you don't like how something is done, do it differently. Make learning exciting by coming up with new ways. Involve others and make the whole process much more interactive. If your learning involves memorizing, for instance, set a timer and challenge yourself to memorize portion by portion within a certain time frame; tell yourself that if you fail, you will have to do ten push ups. You can also record lectures and listen to them with your earphones when on the go. Sometimes, all you really need is to get your limbs moving to prevent yourself from falling asleep. Go for a walk around the block or go do some chores when your eyes start to become drowsy. If this is your preferred method of learning, multitasking may just be your way of showing that you are being productive.

Approach 6:

Make Yourself At Home

Indulge yourself while learning. By that, I do not necessarily mean just with food. Believe it or not, making yourself feel at home is actually an art that can immensely help your learning experience. Having a nice pillow to lean on or a really comfortable chair to sit in can change the whole learning process from dreadful to enjoyable. Set the right atmosphere. Do you like the lights to be dim or bright? Or do you prefer natural light? Burning incense or playing relaxing music in the background also helps. How about decorating your learning space or painting the walls? Whatever you intend to do, make it feel cozy and personal so that the place actually feels like your home. Think outside the box. Study on a massage chair if you happen to have one (though that might be overdoing it.) You can literally do anything that comes to mind. Allow yourself to take your learning personally. Think of yourself as a movie director. You have control of the set and you are to determine the overall mood of the scene, within which you will be the main protagonist. When learning becomes a priority, the sky is the limit.

Approach 7:

Be Temporarily Anti-Social

Peace. You need it. And space too. You want perfect silence and serenity. It is almost as if you need a shrine all to yourself, a place where you know you will not be disturbed nor distracted by anyone. It must be a place that will make you forget about time. Learning is very much like a ritual which should take place somewhere only you know. Pick a location because it means something to you and only you: this will encourage you to return there more often to reconnect with the meaning of the place. Adopt this approach to understand the importance of privacy and whenever you know you can no longer procrastinate.

Approach 8:

Make It Worthwhile

Learning is powerful when you know the benefits. Practice visualization and make it a habit to imagine what it would feel like to have what you desire; this will naturally give you strength to overcome adversity. Why is it worth your time? What is the ultimate goal to your learning? What are the long-term benefits? Figure it all out. Is it to become financially stable? To build your social network? Or is it to further your career? Some people just hate wasting time and would despise the idea of learning for no reason. Most of the time, learning is not much of a choice. Understand the value of what you are doing first, then concentration will happen naturally. Find out what your heart beats for and you will do whatever it takes to keep going. Do it for your relationship, your family, your career, or simply; do it for yourself. Remember, the result of your learning must be lucrative to you in some way and this approach teaches you to specifically recognize value in what you are learning.

Approach 9:

Become What You Learn

Learning is easiest when you approach it without judgment, labels, or preconceptions. When you simply submerge yourself in it with passion and forget yourself completely. Sometimes, that is all you really need to learn successfully. To empty your mind and become a blank canvas, so to speak. Make it a habit to sit outside and watch people go about their lives. Free yourself from all thoughts and enjoy the feeling of being carefree. Realize that you are connected to your higher mind by paying attention to the good vibes surrounding you. If you have a chance, enroll in a meditation course. Learn to raise your awareness beyond flesh and bone just so that you can feel how very much alive you are in spirit. When you adopt this approach, you are telling your subconscious mind that you are done with your self-defeating beliefs, and no matter what, you are fully ready to devote yourself to your learning.

Chapter 4: Where Did Numerology Come From?

Numerology has a cloudy past. Some consider it as a metaphysical science while others state that it's the perception of a mystical and romantic relationship among lifestyle and figures. Numerology is aligned with paranormal and astrology.

The Roots

The rules in numerology have connections about the frequencies of every person. Numerologists begin by evaluating figures that are related to the person's date of birth and name. These frequencies and figures supply perception into the character of a person. In numerology, each single amount has each adverse characteristics and constructive characteristics. Numerology supporters think that its concept determines and emphasize their good personalities.

Historical Past of Numerology Revealed

The past of numerology can be traced back during the ancient civilizations of Egypt and Babylon. Numerology was liked by the early mathematicians. So, where did numerology come from? There is no exact date when numerology came into existence, but others have ideas on where it began. Pythagoras, a well-known mathematician, was credited as the first one to arrange the study. That is why he was called the father of numerology. He believed that the world is constructed within the figures' energy. Pythagoras is also the creator of various theorems which are used in mathematics today.

During the 20th century, a doctor was coined for her contribution in numerology.There is no definitive proof about the real origin of numerology. Several numerologists today state that the earliest record of numerology practice was in Egypt and Babylonia. There are even some statements that Egyptians used numerology to decode their gods' names to avoid their enemies by just pronouncing them.

Numerology is still a mystery for most researchers before Pythagoras, the Greek mathematician and philosopher, believed that everything has numerical values. Even though Pythagoras is widely recognized as the father of numerology, the analysis of each number for symbolic meanings as well as values were practiced for thousands or hundreds of years before Pythagoras claimed the existence of numerical relationships. So, although Pythagoras is not the mastermind of numerology, his studies became the basis for all people using the science of numbers. While traditions and cultures play a big role, the modern numerology serves as the new wave or level of numerology. This science of numbers may not be involved in mathematics, but it still plays a huge part in today's world.

Chapter 5: The Significance Of The Numbers

Because there are so many different forms and disciplines of numerology, there is no solid definition for the meanings behind specific numbers. Really, it all depends on which type of numerology you decide to discover. You will want to look into the different methods of calculation first and foremost; they are as follows:

- Pythagorean
- Japanese
- Arabic
- Indian
- Hebraic
- Chaldean
- Phonetic
- And the Helyn Hitchcock Method

All of these techniques use decimal arithmetic, which means that the system has a base of 10. However, there are other systems which utilize binary, octal, hexadecimal, or vigesimal methodologies. It is important to keep in mind that the technique you use to summate your conclusion will all make you come up with different results. Despite the different disciplines and styles, the basic interpretations are as follows:

1.**One** – **INDIVIDUAL**: This number represents the individual and the self. It symbolizes the aggressor or leadership. In some philosophies, it is representative of Yang. The number one is sometimes used to signify the Root Chakra in metaphysics; and it is said that this chakra (or energy vortex located at the base of the spine) can be stimulated by the color red and the musical note C. It is said that those who have issues with some sort of fear are indeed having issues in the Root Chakra, which can be fixed by performing an action. On a personality types chart, a person who is a type 1 person is described as "The Reformer" because perfectionists who are fixated on improvement (usually in the self).

2. **Two – BALANCER**: This digit is most commonly used to represent balance, union, and partnership. It symbolizes receptiveness, and in some philosophies it is representative of Yin. The number two is often associated with the Sacral Chakra in metaphysics; and it is believed that his chakra (or energy vortex located just below the navel) can be stirred by the color orange the musical note D. Some metaphysics enthusiasts see issues surround this area of the body manifest themselves in the form of the person seeking isolation. The cure: integration (a true quality of balance, union, and partnership indeed). On a personality chart, those who are described as a type 2 personality are referred to as "Helpers" in that they seek to help others who are in

need in an effort to bring more balance and union to the Universe.

3. **Three** – **COMMUNICATION**: The number three usually represents communication and interaction. It typically signifies the trinity, and in metaphysics it is most closely tied to the Solar Plexus Chakra. This chakra is believed to be the energy vortex right below your sternum which is manipulated by the color yellow and the musical note E. Issues in this area will manifest themselves in the form of low self-worth, and should be counteracted by confidence building techniques and the implementation of healthy boundaries. The personality charts describe a type 3 person as "The Achiever" because they are typically somebody who is success driven and who also feels the need to be validated.

4.**Four** – **CREATION**: If you know anything about the way a cell forms or the subject of sacred geometry, then seeing that the number 4 represents creation and self-love will come as no surprise. Four is most closely related to the Heart Chakra (the energy vortex located in the center of your chest), and it can be influenced by the color green and the musical note F. If you are feeling hopeless, that means that there is an imbalance here and you need to seek out unconditional love. The personality charts paint type 4 personalities as "The Individualist" because of their typically inherent need to feel like unique creators (usually artists, poets, eccentrics, etc.)

5. **Five – ACTION**: This number represents life experience, restlessness, and the need for action. It is most closely tied to the Throat Chakra (the energy vortex in your neck), and it is affected by the color blue and the musical note G. Problems will manifest themselves within the sinuses, usually brought on by exposure to negative speech; but the effects can be counteracted by simple positive,

productive, or uplifting conversation. Type 5 personalities are known as "Investigators" because they tend to withdrawal and observe more so than not.

6. **Six – RESPONSIBILITY:** The number six is important in the occult for several reasons, but for general purposes, it is usually identified as the number which represents home, family, and responsibility. Anchored to the Third Eye Chakra (the energy vortex in the center of your forehead), the number six is also associated with the color indigo and the musical note A – both of which affect the person's chakra input and output levels. Problems manifest themselves through general depression, something that can be counteracted by participating in some creative activity that gives you a sense of direction. Type 6 people are known as "Loyalists" because they are steadfast in their loyalties to their cause while being conflicted between trust and distrust of others.

7. **Seven – CONSCIOUSNESS**: By far one of the most influential numbers in numerology, the digit 7 represents thought, consciousness, and spirit. Tethered to the Crown Chakra (the energy vortex on the top of your head) is manipulated by the color violet and the musical note B. It is representative of the divine connection; so those who are personality type 7, "The Enthusiast," need to seek acceptance if they are feeling angry or stale. These people are avid distraction and pleasure hunters; and they are always looking to expand their consciousness. Is it any wonder this number is often referred to as lucky in casinos where pleasure seekers converge?

8. **Eight – POWER**: The number 8 is usually associated with power and sacrifice. Although there are numerous chakras surrounding any sapient being, there is not a specific one tied to this number. However, personality types that fall within the number 8 are known as "The

Challenger" mostly because they typically prefer to take charge of situations without being controlled. These are usually the defectors in our communities; and the number 8 is sometimes thought of as evil in certain occult doctrines.

9. **Nine – CHANGE**: This digit represents the highest levels of change that can occur on the physical plane. Those who are a personality type 9 are known as "The Peacemaker" mostly because they are always striving to be people pleasers, even if that means they have to change or adapt to new situations frequently. Depending on its uses or connections, the number 9 can be seen as a sign of change in the current status quo of a person, place, thing, or idea.

10. **Zero – Void**: Just as you may have already assumed, the number zero is typically associated with a void, a feeling of incompleteness, or a need to feel whole. However, in certain disciplines, the number zero represents just the opposite.

As stated above, the meanings of each number changes slightly based on the methodology and origin of the specific system that is being used.

Chapter 6: Triangle Of Enlightenment

Numerology reduces all multi-digit numbers to the single-digit numbers 1 through 9 with the exception of the three Master numbers 11, 22 and 33. These three Master numbers in many cases are not reduced and have a specific set of attributes that sets them apart from all other numbers. Numerology enthusiasts and practitioners have always been especially excited about Master numbers because, as the name implies, they represent something above and beyond the mundane.

However, in the last couple of decades, some numerologists have adopted all double-digit numbers with identical digits (44, 55, 66 ...) as Master numbers, probably because the mysterious nature of Master numbers tickles our sensationalist nature. This is truly unfortunate, not only because it is incorrect, but also because it diminishes our understanding of the true Master numbers. Yes, it is correct to state that all double-digit numbers with identical digits are powerful for the simple reason that a combination of duplicate numbers, more or less doubles, the influence of the single digit. For example, the number 44 would have double the influence of a single 4, the number 55 doubles the influence of a single 5 and so forth.

However, with the three true Master numbers, their power is not just based on the simple fact that they consist of identical digits, but because those digits are the 1, the 2, and the 3, respectively. In the case of the 11 (a double 1), it has the traits and personality of the 1 twice, and when added (11 = 1+1 = 2) becomes a 2, thereby combining the most powerful male energy (the 1, Zeus) with the equally potent female energy (the 2, Hera).

Considering that the 1 and the 2 are on opposite ends of the spectrum and the sum of their combined attributes pretty much overshadows all other attributes assigned to the numbers 3 through 9 you can perhaps imagine a merging of the strongest, most driven and aggressive warrior, an unstoppable masculine energy, with the supremacy of the most intuitive, feminine, and cunning goddess.

And even that does not reveal the true essence of the 11 Master number: The 11 symbolizes the potential to push the limitations of the human experience into the stratosphere of the highest spiritual perception; the link between the mortal and the immortal; between man and spirit; between darkness and light; ignorance and enlightenment. This is the ultimate symbolic power of the 11.

Similarly, the Master number 22 combines a double dose of feminine intuitive power as represented by the 2, with the ultimate capacity to make dreams into reality; the domain of the 4. And again, the result is not just a range of attributes stacked to impressive potential, but the true essence of the 22: The ability to experience all that the 11 has to offer and apply it to the material world.

Finally, the Master number 33 combines the most proficient powers of expression (the 3) with the teacher and caregiver par excellence; the 6. Its true essence is the final word in spiritual evolution; the Master Teacher.

This, the ability to reach spiritual enlightenment (the 11), makes it a reality in the material world (the 22), then uses it to lift others into enlightenment (the 33), reflecting the enormity of the gift of human life as symbolized by the three Master numbers. Which brings me to the heart of this article: the secret lesson of the 11, a revelation you will not find in any Numerology book or article. Just as Numerology uses adding numbers, it also subtracts numbers looking for the difference between them -- generally revealing what are called challenges or obstacles, and shortcomings you have to overcome. They represent the gaps between the stepping stones, bridges we have to build in order to continue on our path. In the case of the three Master numbers, the gap between 11 and 22 is 11 and the gap between 22 and 33 is also 11. This tells us that in order to move from the height of spiritual understanding as symbolized by the 11, we need to reach an even higher and more rounded experience of divine insight before we can apply our spiritual maturity in the material world, as reflected by the 22. And the final step, the ultimate divine reality of reaching the level of a true Master requires another superhuman boost of divine realization, this one symbolized by the number 33.

Chapter 7: These Numbers Cashed In On The Property Market. You Can Too!

(Case Studies)

In this chapter, I hope to inspire you with the stories of some ordinary men and women, all extraordinary in their own unique way. They have two things in common – they are born with golden numbers and they had also made a killing in the property market. Read the following case studies to find out how they did it.

Why the focus on property? It is one of the surest ways to grow your wealth.

He Owns Six Properties

He is dubbed the "Heavenly Son" because he has the Midas touch. Mr T is born on September 10 and I told him the same thing, so he's come to accept that indeed, almost everything he touches turns into gold. You'd probably have heard of Adam

Khoo, Singapore's youngest acclaimed millionaire but Mr T also quietly made his first million at 27 in business. He now owns six properties, one a HDB shop house in the city with a high rental yield, and said modestly, "It's nothing fantastic. I'm not a risk taker. With my limited resources, I buy what I can afford." He shies away from the limelight and prefers that I keep his identity secret, with the privilege of using his birth data in my book.

These are the notes I made from an interview with Mr T over drinks.

1. Mr T saved $15,000 by waiting one week more for the Fort Road walk up 3-bedroom apartment that would be his first property. "It's all fated." He purchased the property at $275,000 instead of the advertised price of $290,000 in September 1991 and sold it for a cool $1.13 million in 1999.

2. Sophia Court was bought in March 1993 for $476,000. It was a 1012 square feet 2-

bedroom apartment sold for $1.1 million in December 2006 in an enbloc sale. This happened during a year when Mr T vibrated to the power of 8, a number associated with the Wealth Creator. So that explains his lucky streak as it was his big wealth cycle then.

3. But Personal Year 8 can be a double-edged sword as according to Chaldean Numerology, 8 is the "Child of Fate" and you can either win or lose if you bear this number (see how 8 is written - you can be at the top or bottom of the heap). So in 1996, when 8 cycled around to Mr T, he did not make money with his property deal, but he did not lose money either, when he liquidated it this year. Lesson learned: do not buy anything off the developer's plan without seeing it. He stopped investing in real estate as he was caught up with work.

4. In 2010, Mr T bought 4 other properties because he was 'bored'. What an original! He bought one in January, two in March,

and one in April. He quips, "Now I don't go in to the office. I don't have a job. I'm semi-retired." He kept mum on how much the other properties were purchased for, and said it's not always a bed of roses. When business is quiet, he is committed to improving himself by attending courses (that's how I made his acquaintance).

5. In all, Mr T is now a 40-something businessman and has made more than a whopping 1 million dollars from just two properties without speculation but investment in the long-term.

6. He also admitted he struck lottery in the first 20 years he bought his car which has his favorite birth date number association on his car plate - which is also in his email address! This "Heavenly Son" has all the heavenly luck!

He Dreams of Shit and Strikes 4D

Since we are on the subject of enbloc luck, let me introduce you to Mrs T (not related to Mr T) whose hubby is someone who frequently dreams of lying on a bed of shit and then wins big in 4D the following day. Mrs T is born on two golden dates: 17 and 30. Her jaw dropped when I accurately predicted that she donated a significant part of her money to charity. Since her Life Path or Destiny Number is 30, that is easy for me to work out. She has a heart for charity and drives many fund raising events as the President of a not-for-profit organization.

Mrs T bought a private property for $500,000 and sold it for $1.12 million in 2008. She pocketed a profit of over $600,000. I worked out her numbers and told her the deal would be disastrous in 2007 which was a Personal Year 8 as she has the number 8 in her birthday (17 when reduced to a single digit becomes 8). She confirmed that the enbloc deal did not go through with the developer that year. 2008 was a Personal Year 9 for her which symbolized harvest, closure and a fruition of her dreams.

She is married to a man born on January 14, 1947. I told her that her hubby has got the luck of a speculator and would do well in gambling and stocks as he has the golden number 14. She was suitably impressed and confirmed that her hubby indeed has been lucky speculating in the stock market. He also frequently dreams of shit and wins 4D! His wins are of a substantial amount. Like his wife, he is also born with two golden numbers - the other one being 27, someone who wields authority as a leader. He is a high flyer and he is dreaming of his retirement next year which I have also correctly intuited using numerology.

Mrs T's streak of good luck seems to have rubbed off on her daughter who was born on July 12, 1976. This lady who is a number 3 rose through the ranks to become an Assistant Director in the civil service (my advice has always been that 3s would do well as civil servants). In 2009, when she vibrated to a Personal Year 3, she bought a new private property in the East side of Singapore direct from the developer for $800,000. Late last year, the agent who sold her the property, called on her with an offer. An interested party wanted to make an offer for her property to the tune of $995,000. After some negotiations, the place was finally sold for $997,000 in December 2010. Mrs T's daughter made a cool $197,000 profit in one year, just like that! Of course, it came as no surprise that she was helped along by her mini-wealth cycle in 2010 (Personal Year 4).

She Owns A Condo On a $2000 Dollar Salary

When I first met Cheryl at my nail spa, I was intrigued by her good looks and zest for life. She was so lively, she reminded me of my Jack Russell puppy.

One day, our conversations at the spa turned to investments (my fave topic) and I soon discovered that I was talking to an astute investor who responded to the market very much with her gut feel.

After a little coaxing, Cheryl generously permitted me to use her real name and share her story with readers. Cheryl is born on April 17, 1975. She also has the golden number 17, the "Star of Venus", and the Destiny Number 7, which makes her a near genius.

She attributes much of her success in real estate to her elder sister.

In 2000, a Personal Year 5 when Cheryl was poised for relocation and change, she bought Adis Villa, a condominium development along Adia Road with a lucky address of #04-05. She was lucky on two counts. Her sister jointly owned the property and paid the down payment as Cheryl does not earn a fat salary. The place was offered an enbloc sale for $765,000 in 2007.

With the $150,000 she made from the sale of her condo and a windfall from her shares, she placed a deposit for her second property at Sentosa Cove with her sister, a one bedroom studio which they flipped within 2 weeks of purchase in 2009. They walked away with a profit of $80,000 and got back the deposit of $60,000 – with $10,000 extra cash to spend.

Cheryl has since bought her third property, another walk up condominium and gleefully shared with me that she has received two offers for enbloc sale. I shall fondly remember her as the $2000 salaried beautician who owns an old condo. That is her pay and also what she pays for mortgage. Although she claims she did not do well in school, I am full of admiration for her financial knowledge on how to make her money work for her. She is Malaysian and dreams of retiring in style back in Malaysia if she manages to sell her Singapore private property for $2 million when the timing is right.

His Property Tripled In Price

Jack (pseudonym, not his real name), 61 and self-employed, implored me to share this, "Imagine a property tripling in price in about 10 years. Unbelievable! I bought Windy Heights because it was beautiful, spacious and I needed a place to stay."

Jack whose birth date is February 28 bought Windy Heights at a steal - $300,000. That was way back in 1981 and three years prior to that, the developer sold it for $100,000. In 1994, a Personal Year 8 for Jack, he sold his property for a profit at $1.1 million - the 2,500 square feet 4-bedroom property had more than tripled in asking price! After that year, prices dropped to half when we were all affected by the crisis.

Jack is now happily residing at a condominium in the East, debt-free, as the apartment is fully paid up. He has the golden number of 28, a number 1, which denotes success in any chosen field as long as he exercises single-minded focus and independence to act on his dreams.

Chapter 8: The Cosmic Clock Of Gemini

The role of the Cosmic Clock is to show the position of the sun each month and the expected influence on Gemini. Example: Gemini is criticized and feels offended in November, due to the location of the sun in the 6th house in Scorpio. However, Gemini will feel relief and will breathe more easily in December, when the sun moves to Sagittarius in the 7th house.

Gemini's Monthly Forecast

Gemini
 Cancer

Leo
Virgo
Libra
Scorpio
Sagittarius Capricorn Aquarius Pisces
Aries
Taurus
May 21 – June 20
June 21 – July 22
July 23 – August 22
August 23 – September 22 September 23 – October 22 October 23 – November 21 November 22 – December 20 December 21 – January 20 January 21 – February 19 February 19 – March 20 March 21 – April 19
April 20 – May 20
Sun in the 1st house Sun in the 2nd house Sun in the 3rd house Sun in the 4th house Sun in the 5th house Sun in the 6th house Sun in the 7th house Sun in the 8th house Sun in the 9th house Sun in the 10th house Sun in the 11th house Sun in the 12th house

Note: for the characteristics and meanings of the 12 houses of the cosmic clock, see chapter on the monthly forecast

Gemini: Relationships with Other Signs

Gemini 1st house Cancer 2nd house Leo 3rd house Virgo 4th house Libra 5th house Scorpio 6th house Sagittarius 7th house Capricorn 8th house Aquarius 9th house Pisces 10th house Aries 11th house Taurus 12th house

Example: Gemini will be rewarded with a new lease on life and a real experience in the company of Aquarius, but may be disappointed financially by Taurus

CANCER – JUNE 21st to JULY 22nd

Cancer is the astrological sign that represents the areas of home, family, nurturing, and nourishment and those responsible for these areas. However, Cancer is also the sign of the oral phase of psychosexual development, history, memory, money, dress, security and safeguarding, restaurants, and in addition, is connected to ophthalmology, sugar metabolism, the breasts and uterus of the woman, pregnancy, and childbirth. Cancer is introverted and shy, and there are not many famous individuals born under this sign (as contrasted with Gemini, Sagittarius, or Leo, for instance); however, it is difficult not to examine the life perhaps the most famous Cancer of our time in the world, Princess Diana. She was a nursery school assistant before becoming associated with the royal family, which came about as a result of her desire to help the needy and ill of England. Diana was the most photographed woman in the world; and photography, in essence, as a means of recording an image of what was, is Cancer in nature. Diana met her death on account of paraparazzi photographers; however, she was also known to have suffered from bulimia (a Cancerian health problem connected to the stomach). She was photographed with a blind Pakistani child, one of the most famous in the world. Photography, nurturing, assistance, food – Diana's life represents a concrete example of the Cancer.

Ernest Hemingway was also an interesting Cancer. He was a reconstructionist during World War 1, who distributed chocolate and cigarettes to soldiers in the battlefield and drove an ambulance. Harrison Ford and Tom Cruise are Cancers as well. Cruise was born on July 3rd and starred in the movie "Born on the Fourth of July;" the date, of course, being American Independence Day. The U.S.A. is a Cancer.

It is easy to see all of the influences of the moon and the sign of Cancer in the United States. Vested in memories, Americans are unable to forget the assassination of John F. Kennedy and the Vietnam War. Americans landed on the moon on July 20, 1969; and astronaut John Glenn, himself a Cancer, lifted off in his youth and again at age 70+. When speaking of food, the United States is represented worldwide under the golden arches of McDonald's and the logo of Coca Cola. The United States is known to export food to nearly the entire world; and the ideas of "mom, baseball, and apple pie" are synonymous with America. The oral phase, we mentioned….. the newspapers were filled with details regarding Cancer Monica Lewinsky's tale. Complicating the situation was yet another Cancer by the name of Kenneth Starr, who, incidentally, also turned out to be the attorney for the American tobacco companies. Additional oral influences are expressed in Don McLean's song "Bye, Bye, Miss American Pie" and in the image of New York as the Big Apple. The good life in America is symbolized by a martini and a fine Havana cigar.

Cancer is the family. The whole world was familiar with the Kennedy family as a symbol of upper-class America. However, we also must mention the connection between Cancer and breasts, as we can see by the most popular television series, "Baywatch," starring Pamela Anderson, herself a Cancer, who was photographed against her wishes engaged in a particular oral act, details inferred. The image of the blonde, buxom beauty, as in "Baywatch", is as symbolic of the Cancer United States of America as is the nickname, Uncle Sam, connected to the family. Uncle Sam is also connected to Cancer money in abundance. Incidentally, Bill Cosby, a Cancer, earned much fame and fortune with his family-oriented series, "The Cosby Show."

It is of interest that Cancer is connected to pearls. Without a doubt, the events that occurred at Pearl Harbor changed the course of American and world history.

Actor Harrison Ford, in the movie "Blade Runner", deals with the implanted memories of the Androids, as one who destroys and persecutes those with Cancer-like memory that transforms them into humans with identity. Cancer is associated with homeland and patriotism, and another of his films, is "Patriotic Games." Ford is known to love good food and staying at home.

If up until now, we understand that Cancer is associated with oral activities, women's breasts, food, and family and connect Princess Diana, Tom Cruise, Pamela Anderson, and the United States in a package deal; we will now add Tom Hanks to the list. He waged a war of sorts to bring his "Saving Private Ryan" to the silver screen, starring in it as well as in "Big," "Forrest Gump," and "Apollo 13," among others. Tom Cruise appears currently in the film "eyes Wide Shut," in which the most popular scene by far is the love-making with Nicole Kidman in front of the mirror.

Concluding this overview is a philosophical assumption that Islam and Arab culture represent the sign of Cancer – hospitality, clans and tribes, the characteristic foods, the fasting of Ramadan (followed by eating at night by the light of the moon), the veiling of women, the moon symbol over the mosques, and more. Cancer is the sign of Islam, a culture anchored in history, the past more powerful than the future, fantasy and imagination, the world of Suleiman and Achmed.

Marcel Proust, who wrote 3,000 pages of detailed memories, is also Cancer. In his work, called "In Search of Lost Time" Proust eats the Madeleine cake that he received from his mother.

Conception of Time – Time is connected to esthetic motivation, particularly to relationships, as Capricorn occupies the 7th house. Cancer wants immediacy, similar to Aries, which is situated in the 10th house of time, and he is willing to fight for it. Cancer likes beautiful watch and clocks, esthetic and presentable. He feels that time is a battlefield.

Career and Work – Cancers work hard, since the idea of financial security of the family is of utmost importance. Work can be connected to money, hotels and tourism, insurance, healing professions, food, architecture, technical fields, and also the military and sports. Employment is advanced technology is possible, as there is independence and aspiration for individuality on a daily basis. Cancer desires freedom as well as esthetic surroundings at work. Work can also be connected with animals, nature, landscapes, travel, and distances.

Cancer views work as a social event and often makes friends through employment. Work requires much verbal communication, travel, and mobility. Slowly, with much struggle, he is able to pave his way toward professional independence. He is professionally competitive and has a drive to be first. Often, there is a fluctuation between harmony and conflict. Cancer can win awards for his work, and there may be a connection to the search for justice. Work and career are linked psychologically and also in reality to a battlefield, hostility, and competition as to who will be first. Cancer only wants first place. Sometimes, there is an association with children or younger people at work. There can also be work connected with security, safeguarding, and ammunition.

Relationships – There is a connection between the past, memories, and history to present relationships. Relationships are long-term, as Cancers do not like to break-up. In general, it is difficult for Cancer to change or to disassociate from an existing situation. Change frightens Cancer, and separation can serve either to renew or to intimidate. Paradoxically, renewal often takes place through disconnection and separation.

There may be a partner associated with the past, in the sense of fine, aged wine, or an older partner, more inhibited and introverted. Cancer attempts to gain status and position through relationships, and there is the possibility of acquaintance through family or professional connections.

Marriage may be later in life. Pregnancies may be unplanned surprises. There is a sense of shyness, lack of spontaneity, and lack of openness in the partner that Cancer must deal with, understand, and assist. Despite a feeling of time pressure, he feels that there will never be progress without it. There is an idea of fatalism in connection with relationships. Separations and breakups cause great emotional distress, and cause radical psychological changes. Cancer women desire older men with position. Finding them, however, can often be quite difficult.

Sexuality – Despite shyness and introversion, Cancer displays openness and understanding in the area of sexuality. There are situations in which friendships turn into intimate situations, and vice versa. Unconventional thinking and progressive attitudes toward sex may cause surprise and amazement. In contrast to Cancer's shy nature, there is a need for external expression of sexuality, including the need to reveal and expose. The creative side of Cancer may in fact be extroverted – Pamela Anderson, for example.

Siblings – Situations of dependency, victimization, lack of communication may be present, or, in contrast, deep emotional bonds between siblings that defy words. There is a danger of injury to or loss of a sibling. They are complex and complicated emotional, and there is a need to help them. There may be a connection to spiritualism or related healing professions, communications, teaching, or trade. Often, there is disappointment in siblings, and there is a critical and pedantic side that is revealed. The bond often vacillates between fault-finding and forgiveness – in short, a bit confused. There is difficulty in separation and cutting ties, but the communication is never easy and Cancer must give quite a bit.

Children – Children are stubborn, compulsive, and difficult, often acting older than their years and frequently arriving at a later stage in life. They are very physical. There may be hard times and crises related to children, involving the need for constant attention and assistance. There is a compulsive cycle in this relationship. It can reach a level of destruction, rebuilding, and renewal on the part of the parent; or the children themselves may create energy cycles of this nature with their own inner dynamics.

There is a degree of guilt, mutual punishment, and a feeling of limitation and boundary in the parent-child relationship. The future could hold a mutual work association. There may be secrecy or something hidden in connection with children or the relationship, due to the position of Scorpio in the 5th house. In addition, Aries in the 10th house diffuses and synthesizes the idea of the child in this essentially Capricorn house.

Home and Family – The home expresses beauty, esthetics, and design. The father is good-looking, tall, physically fit, stubborn, practical; an economic type or a fighter. He is often gentle but sometimes strict. He may be a military man or employed in structured surroundings. To the outside, the Cancer's parents display authentic harmony, although there may be deepseated marital problems. The mother is more communicative and easy-going, looks younger than her years, and may work with children or youth. Occasionally, she is goading, pushy, strong, and energetic.

Travel, Studies, and Concept of the World – There are failures and problems connected to higher education and a feeling of a cycle that is difficult to terminate. For some reason, the idea of forever is related to education. On the one hand, there may be a mystical or spiritual concept of the world; while on the other hand, practical, everyday, materialistic considerations take hold. There may be deep-seated religious belief. Complications, failures, and problems may be related to travel abroad.

Employment abroad is possible, but there is a need to be careful of health problems. There may be mystical experiences in far off lands or unconventional voyages to special places such as deserts, jungles, lakes, or rivers. Cancer is prepared to go wherever the road will lead. The idea of water is connected to travel, and the idea of "to go with the flow" is central to Cancer.

Denial mechanisms may be present and connected to travel, studies, and the law. Sometimes, under the surface, confusion and lack of clarity exist in relation to Cancer's concept of the world. The overriding philosophy of life for Cancer is the need to take care of people and to identify with them, albeit critically and selectively. Often, the whole philosophy is simply a part of everyday life.

Legal Situations – Legal matters may be associated with work, everyday life, health, relationships, marriage, and possibly connected with esthetics. During 1994 and 1995, a well-known Cancer former athlete and actor, O.J. Simpson, was one of the most photographed subjects in the world in connection with his famous trial. The circumstances of the trial itself were in fact related to "family" matters.

Health – There may be sensitivity in several areas, including sugar levels, the uterus and breasts, eyes, blood circulation, the respiratory tract and lungs, the pelvic region, lower back, and liver.

Mode of Dress – There is a connection to history and to the past, and Cancer is quite sentimental. Shyness, conservatism, and modesty may lead to a style of dress that can be too aging, dowdy, or heavy. A paradox exists, in view of the need for Cancer women to reveal and display their sexuality.

Relationship to the Past and the Future – Cancer represents the past. When the past is seen as harmonious and the future is frightening and threatening, change comes about reluctantly.

Religion – Cancer searches for religious harmony. There may be a connection between religion and relationships. There may also be rebellion and denial of religion, and the desire to defy orthodoxy. Cancer may have been religious at an early age, and the connection may exist with children in a religious setting. There is a philosophical criticism of religion.

Death – For some reason, death is a cause of a certain attraction, linked unconsciously with love, perhaps the idea of love until death. There is criticism and a connection to work and health surrounding this idea. In the chart of Princess Diana, Scorpio in the 5th house (the house of love and romance) led to her tragic death in a car crash following a romantic evening with Dodi Fayed.

Army – Aries in the 10th house indicates the possibility of officer status, command, and authority in the military. In any event, there is responsibility and the bearing of burdens under pressure as well as undergoing rigid tests. A connection exists between the army and status in the achievement of rank promotions.

Relationship to the Environment and Neighbors – Cancer is critical and selective with neighbors. Despite his inclination to educate and advise them, he also takes care of and worries about them, particularly in concerns of health. There will be situations of confusion, disappointment, loss, and inertia from neighbors or the death of a neighbor. Sometimes, there may be situations of sacrifice and generosity in connection with a neighbor. Neighbors may be connected with medicine, therapy, transport, or communications.

Cars – Cancer takes care of and worries about his car, constantly keeping it clean.

He always has something to say, criticize, or educate on the subject. He can hold on to an old car for a long period of time, being reluctant to part with it. Cars can be associated with history and with status. There can be losses and business failures in connection with vehicles, through errors in judgment, due to Gemini in the 12th house.

Sacrifices, Confusion, Illusion, and Places Where it is Difficult to be Objective and Rational - There may be sacrifices, confusion, failure, illusions, and complications in relation to studies, travel abroad, and philosophy of life. Siblings also enter into this category, as well as the car. For example, the inability to give up an old car as something eternal and the loss of its value. Mistakes and frauds may be related to buying and selling, in the course of denial. In connection with the law, justice, and the court system there could be errors, cancellations, and mix-ups.

Chapter 9: Master Numbers 11/2, 22/4, And 33/6

Master Numbers 11/2, 22/4, and 33/6 are higher-octave sounds of the lower base numbers 2, 4, and 6, suggesting great potential for self-mastery in this period. Those with a Master Number 11/2, 22/4, or 33/6 Life Path, Destiny, Soul, or Maturity Number are old souls who have amassed a great deal of spiritual understanding in former lives.

Those with a Master Number hav]e free will to choose whether in their current lives they will use this knowledge to support others and lead to growing planet Earth's collective consciousness and ignore accountability and simply live as their base number 2, 4, or 6.

Here are some exciting details about people with Master Numbers:

They have powerful energies pulsating at higher frequencies.

They've opted to work in some way to make a difference.

Before using their Master Number power, they must resolve the lower tendencies of their base numbers 2, 4, and 6.

Until the age of 45 +, they may not start utilizing their Master Number capacity.

They may choose not to use their Master Number Potential because they have free will.

They can be intuitive and have mental gifts.

To reach their full psychological ability, they must be positive, stable, and rooted.

Anxiety, extreme sensitivity, and/or low self-esteem may affect them.

Strong creators, closely regulated by universal laws.

They can undergo numerous tests, trials, and tribulations, living difficult lives.

Acting with honesty and integrity must be taught.

They are capable of mastering a talent.

They can empower and change lives for others.

They are on the road to personal change and spiritual enlightenment.

Daily sleep, rehabilitation, and a healthy diet support them in general.

NUMBER 11/2

THE INSPIRATIONAL TEACHER

Master Number 11/2 is a higher vibration of Number 2, so it contains all that Number 2 reflects along with the Number 11 added extras. The ability to elevate and inspire others is one of these. Because 11/2 is also the "illumination" figure, 11/2 people are often on a personal development journey to find out who they are and to discover their own reality. They pass on their wisdom to others once this has been accomplished to help them become enlightened, too.

11/2's are considered by all numbers to be the most intuitive. Charismatic, sensitive and enthusiastic, 11/2 runs on nervous energy of high voltage. It is one of their greatest challenges to learn to harness, ground, and manage this nervous energy. When an 11/2 can master their awareness, maintain a healthy self-esteem rate, and conquer Number 2's major life lessons, they start to tap into the 11/2's maximum Master Number strength.

Top 5 strengths

Instinctual

Broad-minded

Inspirational

Elevating

Mediator

Top 5 challenges

Self-doubting

Deceitful

Intense

Delusional

Oversensitive

11/2's make perfect:

Counselors and therapists

Public and motivational speakers

Actors

Artists

Entertainers

Athletes

Musicians

Politicians

Public figures

Life coaches

Clairvoyants

Healers

Spiritual teachers and alternative practitioners

Business owners

Managers and entrepreneurs

Inventors and visionaries

Film and TV producers and directors.

11/2 life Path number

In the event you've got an 11/2 Life Path level, you're already an "Inspirational Teacher," and you're going to walk the path in this lifetime because it's your goal in life.

11/2 destiny number

If you have an 11/2 Destiny Number, in this life, you are expected to become an "Inspirational Teacher" as it already lives in you.

11/2 soul number

If you have an 11/2 Soul Number, your soul is waiting for you in this lifetime to be an "Inspirational Teacher" so it can feel whole.

11/2 Personality number

You are perceived by others to be an "Inspirational Teacher" if you have an 11/2 Personality Number.

11/2 maturity number

In the event you have an 11/2 Maturity Number, you're on the way to becoming an "Inspirational Teacher" from age 45 (or maybe you're already well on your way if you've reached beyond this age).

11/2 current name number

If you have an 11/2 Current Name Number, every time you use this name, you project the sound of an "Inspirational Teacher."

11/2 birthday number

If you have an 11/2 Birth Day Number, you have Number 11/2 personality traits that can guide you along the course of your life and help you achieve your pre-selected destiny.

Born on the 11th of the month

You are highly sensitive and intuitive if you were born on the 11th. You are a deep and caring person who loves to elevate and inspire others. Others can easily hurt you and take advantage of it. You can do big things if you believe in yourself.

Born on the 29th of the month

You become dark, creative, and religious when you were born on the 29th. You may be interested in metaphysics or anything falling under the umbrella of "mind, body, spirit." You are a great therapist and healer with an accessible, loving heart, but you need to learn to love yourself and enjoy yourself.

Number 11/2 meditation

Whether or not you have an 11/2 in your chart of numerology, meditate on the positive qualities of number 11/2 that most resonate with you. Imagine taking on those particular characteristics and visualizing them that will support you in your life. Maybe you want to encourage and uplift the people around you? Perhaps you feel the need on planet Earth to heal others or to raise spiritual awareness? Maybe if you were to live with honesty and integrity and take responsibility for your actions, it would help you on your path? Perhaps you could benefit from taking up practices of conscientiousness?

NUMBER 22/4

THE MASTER BUILDER

Master Number 22/4 is Number 4's a higher vibration, so it combines all that Number 4 reflects along with the Number 22's added extras. One of those optional bonuses is the gift of imagination and the capacity through practical application to transform dreams into reality. 22/4's can see a broader picture of what needs to be done to improve the overall business, company, commodity, program, campaign, trend, culture—and society as a whole.

Number 22/4's is motivated by bridging the metaphysical and material realms and combining their practicality and rationality through their internal wisdom and insight to construct, grow, make, and encourage something of value to all. 22/4's are natural leaders capable of reaching great heights in their chosen field, be it corporate, scientific, health, technological, political, creative, humanitarian, or metaphysical. If a 22/4 can conquer their vulnerability and anxiety, transcend their fear of failure, and resolve Number 4's major life lessons, they begin to tap into the 22/4's total Conquer Number strength.

Top 5 strengths

Visionary

Progressive

Devoted

Dedicated

Idealistic

Top 5 challenges

Stubborn

Overachiever

Dogged

Controlling

Perfectionist

22/4's are perfect:

Business owners, CEO's and managers

Public speakers

Politicians

Spiritual leaders

Inventors

Designers

Scientists

Engineers

Doctors and health practitioners

Alternative therapists

Environmentalists

Public figures

22/4 life Path number

If you've got a 22/4 Life Path Number, you're a "Master Builder" and you're going to walk that journey in this lifetime because it's your goal in life.

22/4 destiny number

If you have a Destiny Number of 22/4, in this lifespan, you are expected to become a "Master Builder," as it already exists within you.

22/4 soul number

If you have a soul number of 22/4, your soul in this lifespan is waiting for you to be a "Master Builder," so it can feel whole.

22/4 Personality number

You are considered by others to be a "Master Builder" if you have a 22/4 personality rating.

22/4 maturity number

If you have a 22/4 Maturity Number, you're on track to become a 45 + level "Master Builder" (or maybe you're already well on your way if you've progressed beyond this age).

22/4 current name number

If you have a 22/4 Current Name Number, each time you use this name, you project the vibration of a "Master Builder."

22/4 birthday number

If you have a Birth Day Number 22/4, you have Number 22/4 personality traits that can guide you along the course of your life and help you achieve your pre-selected destiny.

Born on the 22nd of the month

You are highly sensitive and intuitive if you were born on the 22nd. If you merge your instincts with your logical mind, you have the luxury of additional understanding. You communicate well with others, and when you organize and commit yourself, you can lead large projects.

Number 22/4 meditation

Whether or not you have a 22/4 in your numerology map, meditate on the amount 22/4 positive qualities that most align with you. Imagine taking on those particular characteristics and visualizing them that will benefit you in your life. Maybe you want to be involved in something that helps the community or helps the whole of humanity? You might want to be a pragmatic thinker who knows what needs to be done to make the world a better place and take steps to make that happen? Maybe if you could be more disciplined, organized, and focused, it would help you on your path? Maybe there's a purpose, a business, or a service you'd like to endorse that in some way would benefit others?

NUMBER 33/6

THE MASTER HEALER

Master Number 33/6 is a higher Number 6 vibration, so people with this number incorporate all that Number 6 represents together with the Number 33 added extras. One of those added extras is the ability by conventional or alternative means to heal others. Many 33/6 would heal through a clinical and health-related forum as a therapist or physician would do, while others will heal by their self-expression and imagination in the manner an entertainer, a musician, or a performer would do.

Because of the double dose of Number 3's self-expressive and imaginative power, most 33/6's exhibit artistic abilities. For their overall well-being, positive forms of self-expression are very important. Natural teachers are also due to the presence of number 6, 33/6. Although they may often feel burdened by their duties, their purpose in life is to grow by selfless service to others. If a 33/6 will master their perfectionism, find a healthy compromise between giving and receiving, and resolve Number 6's major life lessons, they begin to tap into the 33/6's total Master Number strength.

Top 5 strengths

Creative

Healing

Sympathetic

Caring

Cherishing

Top 5 challenges

Perfectionist

Overachieving

Critical

Self-satisfied

Humble

33/6's are perfect:

Counselors

Therapists

Health professionals

Childcare professionals

Teachers

Caregivers

Human rights activists

Actors

Entertainers

Artists

Writers

Musicians

Designers and decorators

Healers

Intuitive readers

Alternative therapists

33/6 life Path number

If you've got a 33/6 Life Path Number, you're a "Master Healer" and you're going to walk that path in this lifetime because it's your goal in life.

33/6 destiny number

You are expected to become a "Master Healer" in this life if you have a 33/6 Destiny Number, as it already exists inside you.

33/6 soul number

If you have a 33/6 Soul Number, the soul in this lifetime is waiting for you to be a "Master Healer," so it can feel whole.

33/6 Personality number

You are perceived by others to be a "Master Healer" if you have a 33/6 Personality Number.

33/6 maturity number

If you've got a 33/6 Maturity Number, you're on course to become a 45 + age "Master Healer" (or maybe you're already well on your way if you've gone beyond that age).

33/6 current name number

If you have a 33/6 Current Name Number, each time you use this name, you project the vibration of a "Master Healer."

Number 33/6 meditation

Whether or not you have a 33/6 in your graph of numerology, meditate on the positive qualities of number 33/6 that most align with you. Consider embracing and incorporating unique 33/6 attributes in your life that will help you. Maybe you've got an artistic talent that somehow will help others? You might want to be a healer with the power to ease the pain of another? Maybe your path would be further if you were to teach, heal, or advise those who need your help? Maybe you have a company, brand, or innovation that you would like to bring to the planet that somehow helps others?

Chapter 10: The Destiny Number And What It Means

We all have a destiny, and this is something that we can learn about. Knowing of the destiny numbers can help you learn more about ourselves. Most of the time, when we talk about the numerology of a person, it's usually just about the birth and birth name that is given to the person but their parents, and when they entered into this world. However, both of these are considered equal, but usually the birth name can be seen in different directions. The destiny number is the product of all of the letters in the person's name. You can see the soul urge number that is derived from the verbs in the name, and the inner dreams number is the consonants in the name. You should always consider the full birth name, and you will see here on each of these the nine archetypes that go along with this and what they mean for the person.

Now, this is often called the expression number as well. Even though it's both of these names, it will typically be called the destiny number. Usually, the word destiny is the description of the core element of a person, and it is the number that tells the tasks that you will need to achieve in your lifetime through the name that was given to you by your parents. Your complete birth name does symbolize the opportunities that you have at your disposal, and is sometimes referred to as the potential or destiny that you have. For m any of us, living up to what the attributes of the purpose might not be a good thing, but it is your goal. You can keep this in mind as the spiritual mission, and you can see the field of opportunity. This number will describe what you're about to become.

To get to this number, take each name and separately add up each of the values of the letter, reducing each to a single digit. You can then add the results of all of the names you have to get to the total that you will then analyze. You should not use nicknames, and assumed name, a name change, or take out any part of your birth name. You want it to appear just as it does on the birth certificate. You should go for the complete birth name, and then you can decide what your fate is from there. It's now time to dive into what these different fates mean for the person.

For the number one, you will start to see that the direction of your life is mostly in terms of independence and establishing yourself as a leader of something. You can get the talents to become a great executive or someone in power and you can also do well as a sales executive or someone in a promotional job. You do have what it takes to become a great, original person and be creative with your problem solving and you're inclined to initiate action. You might need to have someone to help with the details, but you know how to make life happen, and you won't' need as much supervision, and you can work with little restraint.

As you continue through life, you will start to expand and get new careers and new inventions, and you will need to develop innovating and ingenuity, you do have the mental power to do this and you will be able to get financial and achievement rewards, and many times you will achieve accomplishments in a business for these efforts.

As you continue, you will be more ambitious and determines, but you will fear the routine of being in a rut, and often you jump the gun because you're scared of what might happen next, and sometimes you will be egotistic and self-centered in life. You're aggressive and it can be hard to live with, but you don't have to dominate to manage this.

For the number 2, your direction in life and growth will be trying to understand people and get a sense of others around you. For a number 2 destiny, you will work well with people, and in general you are a peacemaker. As you continue, you will also grow sensitive to the feelings of others and you can handle complicated situations.

The spiritual potential for anyone with a 2 destiny is very high. You can be inspirational, lead people just through example, and you are an inborn inner strength and awareness leader, and you will do well as a teacher, social worker, or an advisor. You will be aware and sensitive to help the environment, and since your intuition is strong you'll be able to help others with your talents. You are dependent on others and you function better in some group or activity, and you will be able to come more modest as you grow older, and you'll be able to work without achievement. Often, others will get credit for your ideas, but you're not concerned by that because you're working to play as a team. You are cooperative, courteous, and considerate of others, and you have the ability to become a great facilitator, and you will be able to handle details well.

For the number 3, they're mostly growing to be more creative or inspirational. This path will also allow others to be an inspiration to those surrounding them due to the optimism and cheerfulness of this. You embrace the joy of living and want to help others do the same. For most 3s, a large portion of their life will be raising the spirits of others. This can happen in a small level such as through being an entertainer, and it can be inclined as well through writing, speaking, singing, acting, and even teaching. You have some interest in an appreciation of the arts, but the pursuit of these might not arrive. You can also sell yourself or sell any product that might come along too, making you a great salesman, and you're also welcome heavily in sales and public relations as well. You are very mature, and you like to be around people, making you able to be happy and optimistic about living. Most of the time, you are friendly, loving, and social, and you're also very charming and conversationalist, and you can communicate well to inspire others, and the only negative side that you might have is the superficiality of it, leaving you to scatter your forces and sometimes you can be too easygoing as well.

For the number 4, you're driven to have more order, service, and management skills. You will try to approach things in a realistic way and be thorough in your endeavors. You will be willing to work the long, hard hours to get a project done. You will also be patient to detail, allowing you to become great at building, engineering, and even craftsmanship. You will also have abilities to write and teach, allowing you to be more technical and detail. If you're in the arts, you will more than likely be into music, and you might also be into horticulture and floral arrangement. There are also a lot of skilled physicians and even surgeons that have a number 4 destiny, meaning that you will have a life that is full of planning, organization, regulation, and even working through and helping others as well. Often, these types of people can handle a lot of various projects, and some move on to do great things. However, they also have a very moral character and they choose their friends that are part of their high standards. It's hard to hide disappoint with these when they fail to live up to the par that they set.

For the number 5, the growth is present in the changes and the freedom and progression that they make within thought and action. The number 5 destiny is usually one that allows the person to have the characteristic of many talents that allows them to be versatile. They will develop themselves and be able to do a lot of great things well. The main focus of number five is being constructive in the use of their freedom, and the drive to attain and maintain that freedom. For many of these people, the main thing that they must master is the ability to adapt and change at will. As they mature, they will become great at presenting ideas and knowing how to approach people to get exactly what they want. Normally, this will also give a person an edge to help with selling, and it can also give one easy success and it will allow you to work with most people at jobs. For this, a person of a number 5 personality has the ability to be clever, practical, analytical, and a very smart thinker, and they also must learn to accept changes as they go along and don't worry about the past, but instead focus on enlightenment and the future.

For the number 6, the main part of your life will be focused on responsibility, growth, and balance. In this life, you will grow to become more helpful, conscientious of others, and able to rectify and balance any sort of disharmony that comes about. You should be inclined to give help and comfort to others that are in need, and you have a natural inclination to work with the old, young, sick, and the underprivileged. For many of these people, they have a special connection to their home, since charity does begin at home. This is one of the qualities of 6, and it wants to be the best, concerned parent, and one who is a part of domestic activities. In this destiny, openness and honesty in what you do, and in many of the major family relationships you are very close. The main goal of a number 6 destiny is they want to have a happy home life, and if you live up to the promises that are listed in this number, you will get a reward with a lot of luxury and grace to it.

For the number 7 personality, your main focus is searching out the truth. You are trying to become accomplished at analyzing situations, judging carefully, and discriminating, so that little is able to get past the observation and the deep understanding that you have. In this destiny, you will become way more introspective, and you will definitely be a person who likes to operate in a place that is reclusive and it solitude as well. You are also the type of person who can get very involved in searches for wisdom or even hidden truths, and you will become an authority on what you are focusing on. This is usually a technical or a scientific endeavor that you focus on, or it might be something religious or occult. However, that matters very little, since you are pursuing knowledge with the type of vigor that will help you. In this destiny, you can make a great teacher, or because of your desire to be spiritual in this destiny, you might be emerged in many different religious affairs or psychic explorations. You want to study and learn deeply the difficult subjects and look for the hidden fundamentals, operating in many cases on a different wavelength than anyone else.

For the number eight personality, your lifetime will be dedicated to moving up the ladder of attainment in the realm of material, and to achieve financial security and status among the peers that you have. For the eights out there, they are mostly individuals who are very ambitious and goal-oriented, and for many who express the positive qualities of eight, they are usually an extraordinary manager because they are the type of person who can start, change, and complete projects, and they are definitely very dependable and determined as well. The 8 destiny is equipped to develop and grow in a managerial sense, and they have an outstanding chance for organizational and even administrative responsibilities with this in hand. You do have the potential for a lot of achievement in a business or other very powerful position if you're an eight, and often these can be prominent government res. They usually have the skills and abilities to establish and operate a business with effectiveness, and often these types of people are expected to have the financial and material rewards. However, be forewarned not to get too mixed up in the realm of materialism and neglect others.

For nine, the direction will be in benevolent activities, compassion, and even in worldly understanding. You are living up to and growing towards the destiny that is based on following the feelings and even a sense of compassion, and you are becoming more sensitive to the needs of others. For many of these types of personalities, they have a strong will to help others, and many times, they are seen as the "big brother" or a "big sister" type. This type of destiny is one that works well with people, because this is the destiny that has the chance to inspire. This destiny often has a creative ability, imagination, and even an artistic talent, one that is usually latent. However, these are of the highest order that are present in many of these destinies. For many of these people, they excel in advisory roles, medicine, legal, artistic, diplomacy, and religion. Friendships, affection, and love are very important in this, and you should have your personal ambitions kept in a positive way, and you shouldn't ever lose an interest in people, because that's where you're strong. You should be sympathetic and tolerant of others as well.

All of these destinies are right there for you, and you can work to attain whatever one fits you. Yes, they might be hard to deal with, and you might be scared when you look at the size and scope of these numbers and statements, but think about it, if you're able to inspire and help others in the way that's mentioned, you can do just about anything. And remember, this is the destiny that you inherently get, so make sure to keep it in mind, and work to line your energies up to improve the way your life is going.

Chapter 11: Master Numbers

THUS FAR, YOU have been provided an overview of calculating numbers from your date of birth and your full name at birth, and identifying and understanding the Core numbers as well as your attitude. The following is an overview of another area of Numerology, Master numbers, in direct response to the primary question, "How do you know you have a Master number?"

11, 22, 33

Every number in Numerology is significant; however the numbers 11, 22 and 33 are placed in a category of special consideration, which poses the question, "Just what makes Master numbers 'masterful'?" When Master numbers are properly understood and utilized, their profound meanings can prove powerful and productive. The importance is to recognize when the number should be left as a pure Master number and not reduced to single digits.

The Master numbers: 11, 22 and 33, may appear anywhere throughout your Numerology chart, but most powerful in the birth date. They are considered some of the most intuitive, powerful and influential of all numbers, which can be a true blessing—all too frequently disguised as unfortunate, difficult obstacles and challenges.

There is a lot of responsibility that comes with having a Master number. You may own it or dismiss it. The Masters came here with a specific agenda, goal, challenge and gift. How you react to your Master number is entirely up to you.

There is a proper manner of calculating the numbers to reveal whether you have a Master number or not. This is where you should consider having a professional numerologist do the calculations and reading for you. It's where the number is positioned in the name or birth date that gives it the strength, which determines the wisdom to pursue it or not.

The following pages include brief explanation of the meanings of each Master number, followed by the proper method to calculate them.

(11) Master Number

MASTER 11 DENOTES the truest visionary... the Dreamer. You are very intuitive and your number represents illumination—a channel to the subconscious mind, together with insight, sensitivity, nervous energy, and shyness. There is a lot of inner conflict for the Master 11, because of the two 1's. 1+1=2, and since two is ruled by the moon—Luna—if you're not working with the higher frequency and your gift of vision, you literally can turn into a Luna-tic. A person having a Master 11 is not always aware of its power and gifts of illumination and vision, and if you are not taught to focus on a goal that will benefit humanity as well as yourself, it can turn inward and create fears and phobias.

Being a true visionary, you believe you can live the dream and you are able to convince and inspire others to do the same. With your talent of being patient and giving to others, you are very influential. It is said 11's are currently here in force… as a means to energize and stimulate others to prepare for what is to come in our spiritual future. As an 11, you must aim for advancement in your life; you are an educator and you are enlightened. You just have to be fully aware of this reality and work with it. Your interests do lie in the metaphysical world—and the mysteries of our world—and you have the ability to easily realize your dream life.

On the negative side… you may not believe any of this is possible for you, remain "in your head." and ultimately drive yourself nuts.

Barack Obama is a Master 11 Life Path. At the time of writing this book he is the President of the United States, and to honor that position... this is all I can say.

(22) Master Number

MASTER 22 REFLECTS a state of vision combined with action. The builder, you have the power to achieve success where others just think about it or just don't see the possibilities of it.

The 22 is a powerful number, where you are able to more easily turn dreams into realities. With confidence, ambition and discipline, the 22 can create stability through practical actions and strong foundation building. There is a lot of self-control and discipline with 22, because it's two 2's (2+2=4), the 4 is ruled by Ruled by *Rahu Uranus, which rules the intellect. Dreams come from the mind; confidence, ambition and discipline come from the mind.

*Source: Vastu & Numerology and Sanatan Society, Indian Numerology On the negative side, you can be impractical, and when you are not aware of your gift and power, you can inadvertently impose undue pressure on yourself, which subsequently will result in lost opportunities.

Sir Paul McCartney is a Master 22 Life Path. Turning his dreams into a reality... McCartney's music came from his mind.

(33) Master Number

MASTER 33 OFFERS guidance to the world. You are a healer. You are the teacher; the teacher to the teachers and a blessing for and to others. The honest voice, a fully realized 33 is extremely rare. The 33 is a combination of the 11 and 22 = 33 (3+3 = 6) and 6 is the magnet, which draws to it whatever it desires. This master number 33/6 is ruled by Venus, the planet of love—how appropriate that an interpretation of the 33/6 is the mother and lover to all. You encompass all the power, intuition, dreams and potential to fully express yourself to the betterment of humanity and your best benefit. The devotion and high level of sincerity is what a 33 is all about… as well as your determination to seek out understanding and wisdom so you can teach others.

On the negative side, not coming into your highest vibratory level, you will want to **know** it all and want to **have** it all, but tend to expect it be given to you rather than you giving to others or humanity. You may come to **need** a teacher versus being the teachers' teacher.

John Lennon was a Master Life Path 33. He was the teacher's teacher. Lennon sincerely loved people and tried to save the world, stoking popular opinion against the war in Vietnam and myriad other steps toward peace. He taught us so much before his death, and continues to teach us through his music; Lennon's Song

"Imagine" has become acknowledged as an international anthem to peace.

To calculate a master number you add all the numbers together in your birth name and birth date. If the sum total comes to an 11, 22 or 33 you don't reduce it.

Example:

10.12.1953

1+0+1+2+1+9+5+3= 22 this number is a master number and does not get reduced.

The same with the name, all the letters get a numerical value and then added to a single digit and not reduced.

Example:

Mary Jon

4+1+9+7+1+6+5=33

Mary is a Master 33. The number is not reduced.

Chapter 12: Budan – Mercury (Number 5)

People who are born under the days 5, 14 or 23 or the date total by adding all the digits of the date to single number which becomes 5 or as per numerology if the name total gives sum with the number 5 (like 5, 14, 23, 32, 41 etc.) are coming under BUDAN/MERCURY

power.

Number 5 indicates BUDAN/MERCURY and it indicates charismatic power. People born under this number will be a famous personality. This number has the power to attract everyone. People born under this number will easily mingle with others and they will speak out what they have in mind easily. They can't hide anything from others. People can even find out their love matters easily. They want to do which others cannot do and they hate old things and move towards modern things.

They can easily judge the character and habits of a person from their childhood itself. So it is necessary that the parents of the people under number 5 should raise them as a noble person under good company. We can get any job complete from these people because they won't withdraw their help. Self-confidence is essential. There is no defeat for them.

They have to do what they think is right even if others doesn't think it is right. They have Universal Intelligence. They always think about earning huge amount of money from easy jobs. They spend what they earn and will always be rich. It is necessary that they should not gamble. They have to remember that their intelligence is used for completing jobs for the world not for their self profit.

These people may be affected by nervous weakness, gastric problem, mental weakness, Paranoia or fits. They may get small pox in childhood. Doing yoga and breathing exercises will help them.

People born under 5: people born under this number will be attracted to higher ambitions.

They are people with attractive and noble character who respect others. They will teach others and they will lead a divine life.

People born under 14: people born under this number like travelling. They have luck to amass wealth. They'll be successful in business and they are always crowded with people.

Trusting others results in loss. They must be aware of natural calamities. They should protect them from small pox and fever till 14 years. They should not fall in love in youth.

People born under 23: They can achieve anything in the world. They have Raja Vasiyam and Jana Vasiyam. They will get fame even from people who are higher than them. If the name and number matches they can rule the world. If they have noble qualities they will become history's nobleman.

Names and number 5:

You will be ruled by BUDAN/ MERCURY or the number 5 if you have the name total as 5 by adding up all the alphabets numbers making a single digit. **SARNAB** = 3+1+2+1+5+2=14=5

But, remember that the people born under 5 (Either the date or sum of date digits) mostly can have names under 5. Also anyone with lucky numbers under 5 can have their names which will not harm them. It is universal number and fit for everyone.

So, check the numbers and alphabets in the introduction chapter and find your name digits or sum accordingly. If not lucky, change letters or names to good numbers as said above.

Good and Bad Numbers Under 5 (for names by adding all the alphabets' digits)
5 – This number gives charisma, good life,

fame and higher status. People with this number lead a majestic life and will spend a lot. They should try to be hard-working with good focus.

14- This number is good for business. People with this number will be crowded by people and different items. Any type of business will be successful. They will meet lot of people daily. Difficulties and disappointments occur by trusting others. They are endangered by natural calamities. They have to be careful while driving fast. They have to think and act in love and marriage matters else they will be disappointed. This is a lucky number.

23- This is a lucky number. People with this number get victory in everything they touch.

The plans that they lay will surely lead them to victory. They will do things which others can't do. If they don't work hard they will become a normal man. Ambitions will be achieved. They will gain political support and other higher supports. They have to work-hard else they can only lead a lazy but good life.

32- This number attracts different kind of people. People with this number have people's support. They leave new comments without their knowledge. This is a powerful and attractive number. These people will be a famous personality. If they follow their mind life will beautiful if they follow others life will be a failure. Funny speech, intelligence are this number's character. They will face ups and downs. They will be young looking always.

41- People with this number attract people and people will obey their word. They are ambitious people who are successful and world famous. They are driven away be victory and so they do things which are beyond their limits without fear. They will hide their failures from others.

50- They are intelligent people who research things deeply. They are scholars in education.

They will become teachers or businessmen. They will be lucky only after 50 years.

59- They will become a researcher or a humorous writer. They are world's humorous writers. They earn wealth through writing. Even ill-literate people with this number have 22

people's support. They are lucky and concerned with earning money. They may be affected by nervous disorders and gastric problems. So they have to have good habits.

68- This is not very good lucky number but has luck initially and downfall quickly. They will involve in big jobs without fear but feel sad later. Greed corrupts their life.

77- This number indicates effort, self-confidence, hardwork and gives wealth, fame and an attractive life. This number works only if the person has devotion to god.

86- this number indicates a difficult upgraded life and it gives what is deserved. Rich people will aid them by giving wealth and so they will lead a happy life **95**- The number indicates dedicated life, courageous deeds and fame. Wealth is earned by doing modern business. Speaking abilities and popularity will be increased.

104- Courageous life with unexpected turnings. Achieve things. At last It gives fame only.

Lucky Days: 5, 14, 23 are good (Either day or sum of the digits in date). 18, 23 and 27 will also help.

Unlucky Days: There are no specific days which are unlucky. All dates are fit for this number.

Work/Business: People with this number can do any business that comes to the mind. They can work as broker, commission agent, travel agent or helper in any business. They can also be as IAS/IPS etc officer, Chartered Accountant, Maths/ Teaching. The numbers 1, 4, 5, or 9 can be used as sum for the business.

Marriage/ Life Partner: People under 5 may choose 5 or 9. If the sum of the digits is five they can choose 1, 3, 6 or 9. Their marriage date's sum should not be 5.

Lucky Colour: Ash colour.

Lucky Stone: Diamond & Zircon.

Personalities under 5:

NEIL A ARMSTRONG – 05-08-1930 – (5 & 8)

WILLIAM SHAKESPEARE - 23-04-1564 – (5 & 7)

JAWAHARLAL NEHRU – 14 – 11 – 1889 – (5 & 6)

Chapter 13: Take Control Of Your Life

By learning how to live with numbers, you can take control of your life. Be successful, and live happier. It is worth noting that although numbers affect your life, especially your life path number, you remain the master of your life. It is still you who direct the sails. But numbers, just like the stars, can point you to the right direction.

Working with the numbers

Your life path number is only one part of numerology. The truth is that all the numbers can have a significant role in your life. To live in harmony, you need to align yourself to the numbers. This means that you should actively work on them so that you can adapt their positive qualities. For example, if your life path is the adventurous number 5, you can have improvement by working on the qualities of the number 4 so you can have stability. After all, being too adventurous can also be dangerous. Should you open up a business and decide using the power of the number 1, you can supplement it with the qualities of the number 9 in order to ensure harmony in the workplace.

Take note that you do not have to wait for a number to be a recurring number. By having an open mind and putting your knowledge of numerology into practice, you will know that you can always make use of the numbers at any time.

Here is a little, fun activity that you can try.

Imagine yourself as you are. Think of a number that you can strongly associate yourself with. This number may or may not be your life path number. Also, it can be more than a single number.

Once you have associated yourself with a number (or numbers), look for other qualities or traits that you think will make you a better person. Find the number that possesses these traits that you want. Once you know about the number that you need, try to know more about the number and then work on adapting its qualities into your life. For example, if you lack the adventurous spirit of number 5, then go ahead and plan an exciting trip or do something that you have not yet done before.

Do not wait for the numbers to come to you. Learn to live with the numbers and actively work on them.

Use your intuition

The expression or meaning of a number is not limited to what you read in books. After all, it is believed that numbers are alive. Therefore, you cannot just expect to limit their messages to a particular meaning.

You can learn more about a number by using your intuition. It is worth noting that this technique is not for beginners because this takes a developed intuition for this to work properly. If you think that you have a problem with your intuition, then a good way to develop it is by regularly practicing meditation. Any kind of meditation can develop your intuition.

Another effective way that is used in some occult circles to know more about a number is by simply imagining the number. Clear your mind and visualize the number in front of you. Focus on it with an open mind and take note of images that appear or any emotion that it makes you feel. This, however, is quite an advanced technique and should only be used if you already have the right magical maturity.

Numbers change

Although your life path number remains constant throughout your life, the influences of other numbers in your life may change from time to time, depending on the circumstances. This means that, for example, if the number 3 is currently not an issue with your life, it does not mean that the number 3 will no longer be a number that you will have to concern yourself with in the future. Numbers, especially recurring numbers, depend on your current situation in life. As you grow, numbers also grow, until you have mastery of all the numbers. Yet, even then, numbers shall not cease to be present in your life simply because development is a life-long journey. There is always a space for improvement.

Numbers are personal

Like dreams, the meaning of the numbers can also be personal. For example, even if the Pythagoreans believe that the number 9 is an unlucky number, the 9 can be a luckiest number in your life, depending on your experiences. Therefore, if 9 becomes a recurring number, it does not necessarily mean that something bad is about to happen. In fact, many believe that 9 is a lucky number.

Take action

Of course, even if the universe sends you an important recurring number for a thousand times daily, such would not be of any good if you do not listen to it or if you refuse to act upon it. At times, taking the right course of action may not be the easiest thing that you can do. The numbers may direct you to path of change in order for you to grow.

On taking responsibility

No matter how you act, you are the one who is always responsible for your actions. Before taking any course of action, you should think about its possible consequences. Remember that no number will ever tell you to do something silly or evil. However, it is also worth noting that not all messages from the universe can be considered logical or rational. So, the message may not be as practicable as you might see it, at least not in the first instance.

In understanding a number, do not just interpret it in accordance with what most people say in book. More importantly, you should also take the time to reflect on what this particular number means to you on a personal level.

You can create a change

Although there are things in the future that you cannot change, there are also many things that you can change. Realize that the future heavily relies on what you do at the present moment. The moment now is what truly matters. Numerology can help you have a wonderful life that you have always dreamed of.

Mastery of the numbers

True numerology is similar to alchemy. You not only master your life path number but also need to have mastery over all the numbers. Life changes and so do the numbers that you need. Now, mastery of numbers is a life-long journey. You need to master their positive qualities and traits and stay away from their negative properties. Of course, you do not need to master all the numbers if you only want to be successful in life, especially with respect to mere material success. However, you must understand that the true purpose of numerology is not about gaining material things and rewards but to be able to live spiritually and fully. This is what makes it a sacred art. It goes beyond material things.

Mastery of the numbers is not easy, especially when you deal with conflicting qualities. For example, how do you manage the numbers 4 (stability) and 5 (adventure) at the same time? The key is to strike a balance between the two. Now, finding that balance may be hard in the beginning, but with practice, you will be able to be flexible enough and enjoy the benefits of these numbers.

Chapter 14: Wheel Of Fortune

The Wheel of Fortune is a Karmic payback card that spins the destinies of mortals based on the good things they have done in their past lives. The letters TARO appear on the wheel. This is exactly the same word that the Goddess of Underworld holds in The Priestess card. A bull for Taurus, a lion for Leo, an Eagle for Scorpio, and a winged man for Aquarius represent the four fixed signs of the zodiac. The books they hold are wisdom of the ages. The overall symbolism is that while our material existence undergoes ups and downs, transcendental reality is an eternal constant.

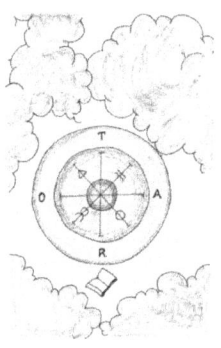

Those under the vibration of the Wheel of Fortune card encounter unexpected developments that change their plans or alter their course. Circumstances will not be under their control and fighting their limitations itself could be a form of limitation. The natives should get ready to experience a new way of life. The apparent chaos can be the beginning of something much better, so be flexible with your plans. Letting things flow will bring good fortune. Events unfold in such a way that it will be impossible to miss the hand of Fate in their affairs.

Name Number 10

Yu the Great was the legendary founder of the Xia Dynasty and is identified as one of the Three Sovereigns and Five Emperors. Yu is best remembered for teaching the people flood control techniques to tame China's rivers and lakes. According to the legend of China's Great Flood, Yu's father, Gun, was assigned by King Yao to tame the raging waters. In 9 years, Gun had built earthen dikes all over the land in the hope of containing the waters. But during a period of heavy flooding, the earthen dikes collapsed everywhere and the project failed miserably. Shun executed Gun and recruited Yu as successor to his father's flood-control efforts. Instead of building more dikes, Yu began to dredge new river channels, to serve both as outlets for the torrential waters, and as irrigation conduits to distant farm lands. Yu spent thirteen years at this task, with the help of some 20,000 workers.

It is said that when Yu was given the task of fighting the flood, he had been married only five days. He then said goodbye to his wife, saying that he does not know when he will return. His wife then asked him what name to give if a son is born. Yu replied, Qi, a character meaning five days in ancient Chinese. During his thirteen years of fighting the flood, Yu passed by his own family's doorstep three times. The first time he passed by hearing that his wife was in labor. The second time he passed by, his wife was holding his son's hand as he was learning his first steps. The third time, his son greeted him and enjoined him to come in for rest. Each time, Yu refused to go in the door, saying that the flood was rendering countless people homeless, he could not rest in his own.

For this engineering feat, Yu has been remembered as an exemplar of perseverance and determination and revered as the perfect civil servant. Stories continue to dwell on his single-minded dedication. In spite of passing his own house three times during those thirteen years, he never once stopped in for a family visit, reasoning that a personal reunion would distract him from dealing with the public crisis at hand.

King Shun was so impressed by Yu's engineering work and diligence that he passed the throne to Yu instead of to his own son. At the end of Great Yu's life, however, his ministers favored passing the throne to Yu's son, Qi, instituting a hereditary monarchy. This created China's first hereditary dynasty, the Xia Dynasty (ca.2070 BCE - 1600 BCE).

Chinese numerology is believed to be one of the earliest forms of numerology. It is thought that the origins of Chinese numerology date back Yu's time on the banks of the Yellow River. The tale that is told is that when Yu found a tortoise shell while working on methods to prevent flooding. This particular tortoise shell, however, was extremely rare, unique and special because it had fascinating markings on it. The shell showed a magic 3x3 square on its back that later became known as the Lo Shu Grid. The Lo Shu Grid was particularly remarkable because every row, column and diagonal on the grid add up to the number 15. The Lo Shu Grid became the basis of Chinese numerology and is still used today in the Far East.

JUSTICE

There is a significant difference of opinion in numerological circles as to the significance of the number 11. Many schools of numerology consider eleven to be an angelic or master number while others see it as negative number that warns of deception, treachery and failures. It is depicted as symbol of a "Clenched Hand", and "a Lion Muzzled", and of a person who will have great difficulties to contend against. The Justice figure is seated with scales in one hand and upraised sword in the other hand. The card suggests you to balance your own inner scales in order to gain equilibrium through reason and discrimination. In this materialistic world, we often spend our life achieving worldly ambitions and material possessions, while ignoring our spiritual development, primarily because we don't want to come out of our comfort zone to make any sacrifices. Master numbers are powerful as they accentuate the vibration of the base number to which they can be reduced. Eleven is a master number that offers tremendous raw potential and it is up to the natives to decide how to use it to the benefit of the society. With your sense of justice, fairness, honesty and compassion you can become a public leader and change the standard of living for the people whose lives you touch. In the lower octave, this card warns of legal disputes, problems in a marriage or partnership. One thing to remember about the Justice card is that it is not about punishment, good, bad, right or wrong. It is about adjustments that may not be pleasant all the time. You should think clearly to weigh up a situation in an attempt to find a fair balance in physical, emotional, social and spiritual planes. Then you will not be disappointed even if the outcome may not be exactly what you have expected.

0

Jesus

Name Number 11

Jesus of Nazareth commonly referred to as Jesus Christ or simply as Jesus was one of the world's greatest religious leaders. The Christian religion was founded on His life and teachings. Most Christians believe that He is the Son of God who was sent to earth to save humanity. Even many people who are not Christians believe that Jesus was a great and wise teacher.

HANGED MAN / TRAITOR

The tarot card depicts an enlightened man hanging by one foot from a tree. His free leg is always bent to form a "4,". He is illuminated and his face is always peaceful, never suffering. He is also the opposite of the World card, 21. With the World card you go infinitely out. With the Hanged Man, you go infinitely in.

Times of great sorrow have the potential to be times of great transformation. But in order for transformation to happen we must go deep, to the very roots of our pain, and experience it as it is, without selfpity or blaming someone else. The symbolism of this number is suffering and anxiety of mind when you are stuck in situations where everything just stands still yet, you just can't do anything about it. Such obstructions usually require great patience and some kind of sacrifice. It may be a sacrifice of wish, dream, hope, a belief or perspective, money, time or even selfhood. Sometimes you may be a victim or you may have to sacrifice a cherished position.

Those who fall under the influence of this card will be presented with an opportunity to see life in all its dimensions, from the depths to the heights. Happiness and sorrow exist together, and when we come to know from experience that the dark and the difficult are needed as much as the light and easy, then we begin to have a very different perspective on the world. By allowing all of life's colors to penetrate us, we become more integrated. The natives will have to open up themselves to the ultimate, and these people will no longer be ordinary human beings. Their insight will become the insight of the whole existence.

Those who find their roots and overcome the hurdles courageously and gain wisdom. And those who do not learn this lesson will continue to suffer.

Anna, Anna, Anna.

No matter in which part of the world, you are from. No matter what meaning "Anna" denotes in your local language and whether you are male or female. If you called as Anna, then the universal number language condenses to numerical value twelve. You are a no doubt a Hanged Man - The Victim.

Anna of Russia was an Empress of Russia. She was victimized by her paramour, Biron. He was determined to govern the nation as well as the Empress and was responsible for a reign of terror in her kingdom.

Alfred Frenzel was a spy who went by the code name "Anna" during the Nazi period. He passed along crucial information to the Communist government in Prague for five years, until his arrest. He was sentenced to imprisonment for fifteen years. "The Ultimate Spy Book" is a best seller novel that was inspired by Anna's true story.

NTR, the matinee Idol of South India who later on became a politician was affectionately called as "Anna". He was backstabbed and overthrown from power by and internal revolution in his own party.

The Hanged Man is definitely a card that brings in trials and tribulations to the native. But one can always overcome their problems with courage and determination. While surfing through the internet, I have come across a thought provoking story that I would like to share with you.

A certain daughter complained to her father about her life and how things have been so hard for her. She did not know how she was going to make it and she wanted to give up. She was tired of fighting and struggling. It seemed that just as one problem was solved another arose. Her father, a chef, took her to the kitchen, filled three pots with water and placed the fire on high. Soon the three pots came to a boil. In one he placed carrots, in the other he placed eggs, and in the last he placed ground coffee beans. He let them sit and boil, without saying a word. The daughter sucked her teeth and impatiently wondered what he was trying to do. She had problems, and he was making this strange concoction. In half an hour he walked over to the oven and turned down the fire. He pulled the carrots out and placed them in the bowl. He pulled the eggs out and placed them in the bowl. Then he ladled the coffee out and placed it in a bowl.

Turning to her he asked. "Darling what do you see?" Smartly, she replied. "Carrots, eggs, and coffee."

He brought her closer and asked her to feel the carrots. She did and noted that they were soft. He then asked her to take an egg and break it. After pulling off the shell, she observed the hard-boiled egg. Finally, he asked her to sip the coffee. Her face frowned from the strength of the coffee.

Humbly, she asked. "What does it mean Father?" He explained. "Each of them faced the same adversity, 212 degrees of boiling water. However each reacted differently." "The carrot went in strong, hard, and unrelenting. But after going through boiling water, it softened and became weak."

"The egg was fragile. A thin outer shell protected a liquid center. But after sitting through the boiling water, its inside became hardened." "The coffee beans are unique however. After they were in the boiling water, it became stronger and richer."

"Which are you," he asked his daughter. When adversity knocks on your door, how do you respond? Are you a carrot, an egg, or a coffee bean?

Are you the carrot that seems hard, but with the smallest amount of pain, adversity, heat you wilt and become soft with no strength?

Are you the egg, which starts off with a malleable heart? A fluid spirit. But after a death, a breakup, a divorce, a layoff you became hardened and stiff. Your shell looks the same, but you are so bitter and tough with a stiff spirit and heart, internally.

Or are you like the coffee bean? The bean does not get its peak flavor and robust until it reaches 212 degrees Fahrenheit. When the water gets the hottest, it just tastes better. When things are there worst, you get better. When people talk the most, your praises increase. When the hour is the darkest, trials are their greatest, your worship elevates to another level. How do you handle adversity?

Are you a carrot, an egg, or a coffee bean?

On the lower octave, the hanged man can be a real traitor who betrays another, a cause, or any trust or commits treason by betraying his or her country. In ancient Italy traitors were punished by hanging a man from his feet which is supposed to be very painful and humiliating.

Raja who is responsible for India's greatest telecom scam falls under this lower

vibration of Number 12.

DEATH

I am Death. That dreads no man,

That catches every man and spares no one;

For God's commandment is

That all to me must be obedient.. .I heed neither gold, silver nor riches, Nor Pope, Emperor, King, Duke, nor Princes,

For if I were to receive great gifts,

I might gain the world.

The early creators of the Tarot have followed the more negative connotations of the number 13 and associated it with the Death card. However, today the interpretation is more of transformation, and warns of the unknown or unexpected if it becomes a key compound number, vowels or consonants in one's calculations. The transformational nature of this card is like burning down an existing house and building a new one on the same foundation. It could be change of plans, place, career or something like a divorce. Just as the sun emerges from behind the clouds; every time we fall, we transform our way of thinking and rise up again to embrace a new beginning.

In some of the ancient writings it is said, "He who understands the number 13 will be given power and dominion and if wrongly used will wreak destruction upon oneself". In 90% of the cases, this card also warns of grave incidents, accidents and untimely death. You should ensure that this number is not cropping in as a soul number, key compound name number or personality number.

Watch your vowels

Guess what is common between Mumbai, Kuwait, Russia?

Can you think of one? Well I see that all the above have evidenced terror in the recent times. The vowels 'u', 'a' and 'i' sum up to the number 13 in the Pythagorean numerology (u = 3, a = 1 and i = 9). It has been noticed that any name (could be person or place) that carries "u", "a" and "i" has been suggesting grave warnings to the future. Caution should be exercised if this combination is creeping in your name as it might affect your health, wealth or relationships in general. To quote a few examples, Arushi's murder is still an unsolved mystery case in New Delhi; Cities like Mumbai and Jaipur have tasted the worst terrorist attacks and countries like Russia, Dubai, Kuwait and Saudi have always been under the threat of intruders.

A. Raja

Name Number 13

A. Raja is an Indian politician. He was a member of the Parliament. The 2G spectrum financial scandal in the Telecommunications and IT Ministry under A. Raja is noteworthy as the largest political corruption case in modern Indian history, amounting to a record $40 billion loss from under pricing to the Government, of India. In 2011, TIME magazine listed Mr. A. Raja's 2G spectrum scam as number two on their "Top 10 Abuses of Power" list (just behind the Watergate scandal).

Sita is one of the principal characters in the Ramayana, a Hindu epic named after her husband Rama. Sita was a foundling, discovered in a furrow in a ploughed field and was adopted by a king from today's Nepal. Sometime after the wedding, circumstances forced Rama to leave his kingdom. Sita willingly renounced the comforts of the palace and joined her husband in braving exile. King Ravana abducted Sita from the forest and held her as a prisoner in one of his palaces in today's Srilanka. During her captivity for a year in Lanka, Ravana expressed his desire for her; however Sita refused his advances and struggled to maintain her chastity. Sita was finally rescued by Rama. The couple came back to Ayodhya, where Rama was crowned king with Sita by his side. While Rama's trust and affection for Sita never wavered, it soon became evident that some people in her kingdom could not accept Sita's long captivity under the power of Ravana. Sita was thus forced into exile a second time; she was not only alone this time but also pregnant. She was rescued by the sage Valmiki. He gave her refuge in his hermitage, where she delivered twin sons. In the hermitage, Sita raised her sons alone, as a single mother. They grew up to be valiant and intelligent, and were eventually united with their father. Once she had witnessed the acceptance of her children by Rama, Sita sought final refuge in the arms of her mother to release from an unjust world and from a life that had rarely been happy. Even today, Sita is esteemed as the standard setter for wifely and womanly virtues for all Hindu women.

Chapter 15: The Principles Behind Predictions

Numbers in the date of birth are not static, but dynamic. They produce actions and results. Every number in our date of birth comes repeatedly in cycles, influencing our life, fortunes or growth, either beneficially or adversely.

The nine numbers, 1 to 9, correspond to nine different planets. In the Vedas, they call them the Navagrahas.

1 – Sun	2 – Moon	3 – Jupiter
4 – Uranus	5 – Mercury	6 – Venus
7 – Neptune	8 – Saturn	9 – Mars
0 – Pluto		

Even though 0 does not occur alone, it affects the person when it occurs by itself in different phases of life.

As per Vedic philosophy, the fortunes of a person change drastically every 9 years because of the navagrahas or nine planets.

This means that before every 9-year cycle begins, whatever maybe the net assets or status of one's fortune, it changes gradually and steadily, creating a new, changed or altered status or fortune or assets by the end of the ninth year.

For example, a person's 9-year cycle begins at the age of 27, when he may be worth 10 million or maybe a manager in a firm. At the end of age 36, the position of this person may have changed to his having 20 million, or being a Senior Vice President, or else to having 5 million and maybe without a job.

What accounts for the rule of the 9? As per Vedic mathematics, amongst all the numbers from 0 to 9, Number 9 is considered to be a true number.

Here are the reasons why:

1. When 9 is added to any number, the result will also be the same number.

5 + 9 = 14. Add 1 + 4 = 5

14 + 9 = 23. Add 2 + 3 = 5

(Where 1 + 4 = 5)

2. When the number 9 is subtracted from any number, the result will still be

the same number.

16 – 9 = 7

(Where 1 + 6 = 7)

56 – 9 = 47. 4 + 7 = 11. 1 + 1 = 2

(Also, 5 + 6 = 11 = 1 + 1 = 2)

3. When a number is multiplied by 9, the result is the same number.

9 × 5 = 45. 4 + 5 = 9

9 × 8 = 72. 7 + 2 = 9

4. When any number is divided by 9, the remainder will be equal to the total

of the number.

56 divided by 9 = 56 – 54 (9 × 6) = remainder 2

(5 + 6 = 11 = 1 + 1 = 2)

82 divided by 9 = 82 – 81 (9 × 9) = remainder 1

(8 + 2 = 10 = 1 + 0 =1)

Thus, whether we add, subtract, multiply or divide by 9, the value of the number remains the same. So number 9 is called the digital root of a number.

This is also why every 9 years, the fortunes of a person change progressively or adversely. In these 9 years, a person may undergo 3 years of a rough patch, or 3 years of growth, or 3 years of a plateau. These three periods can interchange in any manner. What this means is that no one has got either good luck or bad luck only from birth to death in one vertical line.

Fortunes fluctuate like a sine curve

Because 9 years is too long a period, we reduce it to a 1-year cycle. The underlying philosophy is the same for 1 year too — that is, the net result of the fortune at the beginning of the year will be different at the end of the year. But again, the progress need not be in one vertical line, but will be just like a sine curve.

In most instances, people come to consult a numerologist regarding the present state of affairs. For this purpose, we can bring down the 1-year cycle to a 1-month cycle. In this way, it is possible to calculate by the hour, and such is the exhaustive scope of this fascinating subject of numerology that we will be dealing with in the coming chapters.

Chapter 16: Karmic Lessons

We have spoken about the various evident characteristics in a person. But now, let's have a look at some of hidden and deeper desires and ambitions that a person may not be aware of. If you want to let yourself go free, you need to turn these unconscious traits into conscious ones. You must access these traits in the deepest realms of your mind in order to be able to control your life. Until you do that, you will always be a slave to your unconscious desires.

The Karmic Lessons Chart

The basis of Numerology is the fact that we come into this world with both strengths and weaknesses. The Karmic Lessons signify areas that you are weak in. You need to work on these areas. You can have more than one Karmic Lesson.

Each letter in your name has a specific number. Some letters have the same number. Also, a name has repetitive numbers. Hence, certain numbers will be repeated in a name while others will be missing. These missing numbers indicate your Karmic Lessons. Karmic Strength occurs when a number shows up more than once. The numbers point to traits and talents you may possess. So not having a number could indicate a lack of a trait or talent while frequent repetitions of a number indicate a stronger sense of that characteristic or talent. Missing talents can always be learnt during your lifetime. Just because they do not show up in your name doesn't mean you cannot master them.

If you have three or more numbers missing, it is essential that you focus on overcoming obstacles that come in the way of you goals and ambitions. The kind of energy that is suggested by your name gives you the ability to achieve great things in a specific field or part of life. However, to make use of that ability, you need to overcome any obstacles that you might face. In order to do that, you need the perseverance to keep trying.

How to Calculate Your Karmic Lessons

Karmic Lessons can be calculated by finding the missing numbers amongst the letters of your full name that you are given at birth.

For example, in the name Joe Hamilton, we see that the following numbers are present:

J- 1

O- 6

E- 5

H- 8

A- 1

M- 4

I- 9

L- 3

T- 2

O- 6

N- 5

You can also write the numbers as given below:

1 found 2 times

2 found 1 time

3 found 1 time

4 found 1 time

5 found 2 times

6 found 2 times

7 not found

8 found 1 time

9 found 1 time

In the above name, we find that all the numbers are represented except 7. Therefore, Joe has one Karmic Lesson: 7.

Meaning of the Karmic Lessons

Let's now discuss about the meaning behind each Karmic Lesson.

Karmic Lesson 1

If you have this Karmic Lesson, you need to take a more active role in your life. You need to be more determined. The will to succeed and prove yourself needs to be stronger. You need to be able to stand up for what you think is right. This can be done only if you have the will to do it. You can also be indecisive. You need to learn to overcome this particular trait and take more decisions in your life. Life will throw many strong willed people in your direction. The task will be to stand out amongst their loud voices. You will need to be more independent if you want your voice to be heard. If you can't do this, you will be forever be suppressed by the stronger people around you. To avoid that you need to be more forceful. You should learn not to care about what others think and also improve your self-confidence. You may be meek and timid but if you continue to be like that, you will get nowhere especially with all the strong people that life sent your way. In order to make others listen to you, you need to believe in yourself. So, work on your self-confidence.

The effect of this particular Karmic Lesson is diminished if you have at least one more 1 among your core numbers.

Karmic Lesson 2

You lack the ability to be tactful and diplomatic and this can often lead to your downfall. You also like the praise and spotlight. You need to learn to stay in the background when essential and let others take credit when they have to. Team spirit is the most important quality that you need to learn. You can often be oblivious to the feelings and emotions of other people. You will often find yourself in situations where you need to work with others patiently to achieve the goal you want.

You can diminish the effect of this Karmic Lesson if you have another two among your core numbers.

Karmic Lesson 3

You can be extremely self-critical. Every time you do something commendable, you find some obscure detail that you find embarrassing and focus on that rather than the amazing feat you achieved. You have this high standard of perfection that you cannot achieve. You need to relax in life and let yourself free once in a while. You need to acknowledge the fact that your critical thinking must be controlled. You need to realize that this critical thinking will not always help you. Otherwise, it will only prevent you from doing something you love or from having fun. You are too serious and practical. You need to learn to be more optimistic. You need to enjoy life and share this joy of living with others. Life will often put you in situations where you need to use your imagination or rely on communication.

These two areas are your weaknesses and life will look to test you in these areas.

You can reduce your Karmic Lesson effect if you have at least one more 3 in your core numbers.

Karmic Lesson 4

You are confused with how your life is going. You need to ensure that there is an ordered way in how you tackle life. If you fail to do so, you might feel lost and clueless. You have a problem discovering the ideal job for yourself. You also doubt your own capabilities. Impractical and chaotic are sometimes used to describe you. You tend to search elsewhere for the answers to your life problems, rather than look into yourself. You are enthusiastic about new things but often lose interest very quickly. After a point of time, the new task or work becomes just like any other work and this begins to bore you. You feel the need to put in a lot of effort without feeling excited about it. This makes you give up soon. Your concentration needs to improve.

Like the others, the effects are decreased if you have at least another 4 among your core numbers.

Karmic Lesson 5

You tend to have a fear of living your life. You need to be more adventurous. Take any opportunity that comes your way. Use it to travel the world and meet new people and get to know new customs. Be social. You need to embrace new experiences and expand your vision. Life will give you situations that will need you to adapt to various circumstances. Use these situations to overcome your inflexibility and rigidity. You need to take things with the flow and be open to change and growth. The best way to learn something is to experience it.

The effects can be reduced by having at least one more 5 in your core numbers.

Karmic Lesson 6

You are against commitment and have issues being responsible to others. You just cannot bring yourself to commit to long-term relationships or marriage. You are incapable of showing emotion and this one problem you need to work on. There are times when you feel all alone despite having people around you. This is why you often put a barrier between you and other people. You form relationships but always maintain a distance by putting up a façade of emotion yet remaining aloof. This will make all your relationships superficial. You need to understand the importance of having genuine relationships. The lesson of giving and sacrificing for the people you care about is one that you need to learn. This is the only way you will find lifelong friendship or love.

If you have another 6 in your core numbers, you can decrease the effects of this Karmic Lesson.

Karmic Lesson 7

You need to focus your talent and skills in a particular field. In order to perfect a skill, you need the determination and inclination to do so. This is what you lack. You should be your own critic without putting yourself down. Taking things at their face value does you no good. A superficial knowledge will prevent you from achieving your best. You will not be able to experience the satisfaction of utilizing your complete potential.

Similar to the others, you need to have at least one more 7 to reduce the effects.

Karmic Lesson 8

You will be a good businessperson and you will always attract money. However, you will face a lot of fluctuation in your finances because of your reckless handling of the resources give to you. You work independently and do not like it when people tell you how to do things. This makes it difficult for you to work under a boss. This is because of your obstinate and know-it-all attitude. You will also need to work to keep the money you attract. You tend to make money but somehow the same money slips through your fingers. You will be forced to work on your weaknesses such as being efficient.

You can reduce the effects by having more than one 8 in your core numbers.

Karmic Lesson 9

If you have this Karmic Lesson, you need to learn to be more broadminded and understanding of other people. You also need to learn to be compassionate and generous. You need to patient with the problems that others face. There will be instances in your life where you will have to let your ambition go in order to do something good. You also need to broaden your outlook of life. For the most part, you are oblivious to how much of an influence you have on your own destiny and others too. Hence, you tend to think twice before helping people.

The effects of this Karmic Lesson are reduced by having more than one 9 among your core numbers.

Chapter 17: Using Your Numbers To Win!

Remember the number of times you have lucked upon great buys or won a prize or some bucks at the casino? Well, you would call it "your day" because of the belief that luck is arbitrarily spread but numerologists wouldn't concur. Your winning, just like anything else, was not a result of a series of random events, but a deliberate ordering of numerical events that added up to the number or numbers that are lucky to you.

Conclusion

Thank you for purchasing the book.

You have been given a thorough explanation on how you can use numerology to predict your future or anybody else's future. Make sure you practice on yourself before you experiment the reading for someone else.

Take baby steps and you will be fine!

Thank you once again.

www.ingramcontent.com/pod-product-compliance
Lightning Source LLC
Chambersburg PA
CBHW072008070526
44583CB00015B/1384